How to Beat Worry

Dr David Delvin is director of the Medical Information Service, and one of Britain's best-known media doctors. He trained in medicine at King's College Hospital, London, and subsequently worked at hospitals in Sussex, Kent and the West Indies. After becoming a member of the Royal College of General Practitioners, he established a successful career in writing and broadcasting about medicine and surgery. He has now appeared in over 900 medical TV programmes. His work has received awards from the American Medical Writers' Association and the Medical Journalists' Association. He has also been Consumer Columnist of the Year and he was awarded the *Médaille de la Ville de Paris* by Jacques Chirac in 1983. His last book for Sheldon Press, *Backache: What you need to know* (2009) won the Medical Journalists' Association Tony Thistlethwaite Award for excellence in communicating medical and health information in a book for the lay reader.

Overcoming Common Problems Series

Selected titles

A full list of titles is available from Sheldon Press,
36 Causton Street, London SW1P 4ST and on our website at
www.sheldonpress.co.uk

Overcoming Common Problems Series

Overcoming Common Problems Series

Overcoming Common Problems

How to Beat Worry and Stress

DR DAVID DELVIN

sheldon **PRESS**

First published in Great Britain in 2011

Sheldon Press
36 Causton Street
London SW1P 4ST
www.sheldonpress.co.uk

British Library Cataloguing-in-Publication Data

A catalogue record for this book is available from the British Library

ISBN 978-1-84709-129-1

1 3 5 7 9 10 8 6 4 2

Typeset by Fakenham Photosetting Ltd, Fakenham, Norfolk
Printed in Great Britain by Ashford Colour Press

Produced on paper from sustainable forests

Contents

Dedicated to Mr John Skinner FRCS, who pulled me through

Acknowledgements

For their help with this book, many thanks to:

Mrs Christine Delvin, Psychotherapist
Professor Jeffrey Aronson, President Emeritus, British Pharmacological Society
Dr Tony Richards FRCP
Dr Mike Knapton, Associate Medical Director, British Heart Foundation
Dr Frank Tallis, Clinical Psychologist
Ms Patsy Westcott, Health Journalist

Introduction

I imagine that you're reading this book because you're in a state of stress, or have some other form of psychological or emotional condition – and I want to help you.

Psychological distress is extremely common. It can take various forms, for instance:

- stress
- anxiety
- worry
- disturbing bodily symptoms.

In this book, you will find chapters on each of the above. However, the important point that I'd like you to appreciate right now is that *they are all aspects of much the same thing* – namely, the brain being subjected to circumstances that it can't cope with.

When this happens, your nervous system starts producing various powerful compounds, known as 'hormones' or 'chemical messengers'. And very often the hormones cause alarming, but perfectly genuine, symptoms – symptoms that may well throw your life into chaos.

In addition, further scary symptoms can be caused by changes in your body chemistry, and particularly by the level of carbon dioxide in your blood. None of this is imaginary.

When the brain can't cope

People use different terms to describe this rather frightening state of affairs, and the words they employ depend to some extent on how old they are. It's often a generational thing. So, the more elderly may talk about 'suffering from nerves' or 'being nervy' or 'living on my nerves'. Middle-aged people often say that they're having problems with 'anxiety' or 'worry'. Younger men and women will state that they are 'stressed out' or 'badly stressed' – terms that were scarcely used until the last quarter of the twentieth century.

But whatever you choose to call your situation, the fact is that your poor, tired old brain is finding everything a bit much for it. So it reacts by getting the body to produce those chemical compounds we mentioned, particularly adrenaline.

Please note that you have little or no conscious control over the production of hormones, so you can't be blamed for any effect that they may have. So there is no point in anyone barking at you: 'Pull yourself together!'

Unfortunately, these chemicals and hormones cause all sorts of symptoms, and can have the effect of making you feel pretty awful. Such feelings are *not* imaginary. So don't believe anyone who tells you that 'it's all in the mind'. It isn't.

Effects of hormones

What are the effects of 'distress chemicals' such as adrenaline? Well, they can be very varied. They may make you feel:

- tired
- 'jumpy' or nervous
- frightened
- unable to concentrate
- panicky
- irritable.

And they may produce any of these perfectly genuine physical symptoms:

- a fast heartbeat
- thumping in the chest
- tightness in the chest
- rapid breathing
- aches and pains
- dizziness
- a lump in the throat
- churning and/or a feeling of 'butterflies' in the tummy
- rumbling stomach and intestines
- bloated abdomen
- nausea
- bowel disturbances.

These complaints are very common, and there's a lot more about them in Chapter 6.

Every day, hundreds of people walk into their doctors' surgeries and complain about one or other of the above symptoms. And, in many cases, the GP sighs inwardly, and thinks to herself: 'Here we go again'.

Within a few minutes, this GP may well be reaching out for an investigation form, so as to order some lab test or X-ray which – she is almost sure – will come back reported as 'normal'. (Regrettably, ordinary lab tests cannot measure the levels of things like adrenaline.)

Alternatively, she may reach for her prescription pad, and write out the name of a popular tranquillizer, hoping that this drug will keep the person's symptoms at bay for a few months.

But it probably won't. As we'll see in this book, tranquillizing drugs and sedatives are not, as a rule, the answer to symptoms of psychological distress.

However, there are often ways of dealing with these symptoms. To find out what these ways are, please read on ...

1

It's *not* 'all in the mind'

So you've suffering from stress or anxiety or worry – and doubtless you've had lots of unpleasant symptoms. You've probably been to the doctor about them. Maybe you've had tests, and no one has really been able to find anything physically wrong with you.

You aren't imagining it

So, are your symptoms 'all in the mind'? I don't think so.

Let me tell you a story. Suzie Jenkins had felt 'stressed out' for many months. She had a demanding job, and she was trying to bring up her two children on her own. Her husband had left her the previous Christmas, and quite often there were delays in the arrival of the monthly cheque that he was supposed to send her.

Then she began to experience troubling physical symptoms. In particular, she had bouts when her heart started to beat very fast and very hard. She told her best friend: 'It goes at about 100 a minute, and it feels as though it's going to burst out through my ribs.'

She went to her doctor. The GP examined her, and listened to her heart and lungs with his stethoscope – but he could find nothing amiss. But the attacks persisted. So the doctor decided to arrange an electro-cardiogram (ECG), which is the well-known electrical test on the heart. The results came back as 'completely normal'.

But Suzie was still troubled by the thumping. In an effort to find out what was wrong, the doctor ordered blood tests, including one for thyroid gland problems. However, all of these investigations were reported as normal too.

The palpitations continued. In some desperation, the doctor sent Suzie for a chest x-ray. It too turned out to be perfectly OK.

So what on earth was going on? Were Suzie's attacks of fast heart-beats all in her mind?

No, they weren't. Indeed, if anyone had taken her pulse during an attack, they'd have found that her heart genuinely *was* batting along at 100-plus beats per minute – although soon afterwards the rate went back to normal.

What was really happening was that because of the stress, anxiety and worry that she had been subjected to, Suzie's body was producing far too much adrenaline, plus a related hormone called 'noradrenaline'.

Adrenaline

Now what's adrenaline? You often hear people talking about it these days, particularly in the media. For instance, an athlete may be quoted in the newspapers as saying: 'I came into the home straight, and then the adrenaline really kicked in.' Or a film star may tell a journalist: 'When I went up to collect my Oscar, I had *such* a massive adrenaline rush.' Also, fans of dangerous sports may refer to themselves as being 'real adrenaline junkies'. By this they mean that they like getting extremely excited, particularly in perilous situations.

Now in reality it's unlikely that many of these people really know what adrenaline is, but they're correct in thinking that they produce a lot of it when they're in exciting or dangerous situations.

So what is it? Well, adrenaline is a hormone that genuinely does have quite dramatic effects on the body. These are its main actions:

- It speeds up the pulse rate and heart rate.
- It makes the heart beat more strongly.
- It raises the blood pressure.
- It opens up the pupils of the eyes (giving people a wide-eyed, staring look).
- It diverts blood to the muscles, and away from places where it's not immediately needed.
- It narrows the blood vessels (i.e. tubes) in the skin, often making people look very pale (hence the phrase 'the blood drained from her face').
- It increases sweating.

Note particularly those first two points: adrenaline accelerates your heart rate, and also makes your ticker beat more strongly.

Could those two actions have any relevance to Suzie Jenkins's case? Most definitely! But we'll come back to her in a minute.

First of all, let's be clear about what adrenaline actually is. (Incidentally, if you're American you may perhaps know it by the US scientific name of 'epinephrine'.) It is a hormone – that is to say, a chemical messenger. It's produced by your two adrenal glands. They are located just above your kidneys, as you can see from Figure 1.

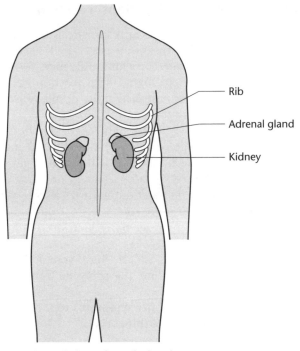

Rib

Adrenal gland

Kidney

Figure 1 Location of the adrenal glands

The adrenal glands are tiny. Each of them is about the size of a Brazil nut, and weighs only about the same as a teaspoonful of sugar (5 grams). The important thing to grasp is that they are very much under the control of the 'unconscious' part of your brain.

So if you are under stress, or frightened, or simply excited, that part of your brain immediately sends messages to your adrenal glands, telling them to pour out more adrenaline.

Why? Simply because adrenaline prepares the body for urgent *action*. By getting the heart to beat faster and more strongly, and by opening up the tubes that carry blood to the muscles, adrenaline gets you ready for battle – or perhaps for running away. So, when one of your distant ancestors saw a dangerous animal, like a wild boar or a sabre-toothed tiger, galloping towards him, his adrenals instantly started pouring out adrenaline. Result? Within seconds, his body was ready to take on the savage creature – or else to run like blazes.

The 'fright, fight, flight' reaction

This natural outpouring of adrenaline is known as the 'fright, fight, flight' reaction, and that sums things up pretty well. Please note that this reaction is *not* under your conscious influence. So your mind doesn't say: 'Oh, let's do a fright, fight, flight reaction here.' No, the message to your adrenal glands is sent by quite primitive parts of your brain, over which you have no real control.

Now the adrenaline-induced 'fright, fight, flight' reaction is all very well on a battlefield, or if you're about to run the 100 metres, or if you're going out to play in a Cup Final. It will instantly get your body ready to deal with all of these situations. But in ordinary day-to-day life, what you do *not* need is frequent outpourings of adrenaline. After all, if you're trying to get on with your job, or collect the children from school, or see the bank manager about your overdraft, you don't require an 'adrenaline rush'.

What you need is to keep calm, isn't it? But if your adrenals are suddenly producing loads of adrenaline, the probable result is that your heart will start beating wildly.

And you may get all sorts of other symptoms too. These vary a lot from person to person, but include things like:

- turning pale
- trembling
- gasping for breath
- feeling groups of muscles tighten up, particularly in the throat
- being unable to speak.

In some people, adrenaline actually makes the hair stand on end! This is thought to be a primitive reaction that made early humans look more fearsome to anyone who was attacking them. You've probably seen a similar phenomenon in cats when they're scared.

Adrenaline also suppresses certain activities of the body, because of the fact that they are not needed for fighting or running away. Thus, adrenaline depresses the digestive processes. It also interferes with sexual function, and will make it difficult for a man to get a good erection, or to continue intercourse for any length of time. That's why anxiety and stress tend to cause erectile dysfunction (ED) and premature ejaculation (PE) – this is covered in Chapter 4.

But coming back to Suzie Jenkins, her situation could be summed up in these four points:

1 She was trying to cope with a lot of stress and worry.

2 The unconscious part of her brain responded to these factors by sending a message to her adrenal glands.

3 Her adrenals started pouring out bursts of adrenaline into her bloodstream.

4 The effect of the adrenaline was that her heart started to beat like a very fast steam-hammer – and she thought it was going to 'burst out' through her ribs.

Very fortunately, in Suzie's case what happened next was that a therapist friend showed her one of the effective ways of defeating stress and anxiety, by practising deep relaxation through breathing exercises, three or four times a day (see Chapter 9). The result was that her brain felt less stressed, and over a period of weeks it gradually stopped sending those 'alarm messages' to her adrenal glands.

Therefore, there were no more inappropriate outpourings of adrenaline, and Suzie Jenkins had no further attacks of palpitations. So I hope you can see now that these thumpings in her chest were definitely *not* all in her mind. They were a perfectly genuine physical response to the pressures to which her brain had been subjected.

For completeness, I should add that under the influence of stress, anxiety and worry, the adrenal glands do turn out a couple of other hormones that produce bodily symptoms. Let's have a quick look at them.

Noradrenaline (norepinephrine)

Noradrenaline is another stress-induced hormone. Chemically, it is closely related to adrenaline.

A lot of it is stored in the endings of what are called 'the sympathetic nerves'. These are not really under your conscious control, and they are often activated by stress.

Noradrenaline is also produced by the tiny adrenal glands, and contributes to the 'fright, fight, flight' reaction. Among its main actions are:

- It shifts blood flow into the muscles, and away from other parts of the body.
- It can increase the heart rate.
- It promotes the release of glucose into the bloodstream, so raising the blood sugar.

In addition, when you are subjected to a stress of some kind, noradrenaline is released from an area in the base of the brain. There, it acts as a sort of 'pep up' hormone on your mind, making you highly alert and ready for muscular action. That's fine if you are going out to run a race, or stepping into a boxing ring! But in everyday life, you don't actually need to have all this mental stimulation. So stress-induced release of noradrenaline tends to make you feel nervous and jumpy.

One way of dealing with this sort of jumpiness and nervousness is to do some physical activity. This has various good effects, including 'burning up' the noradrenaline. I have had a number of patients who learned that when they were feeling 'up-tight', the best thing to do was to go out for a run, or have a vigorous work-out at the gym.

Incidentally, exercise has the additional benefit of stimulating your brain to secrete endorphins. These are the body's natural 'happiness promoters' or 'tranquillizers', and many people find that within 10 or 20 minutes of starting to exercise, they can feel the calming effect of endorphins on the mind.

Cortisol

Under conditions of stress, the hormone called cortisol is released from the outer part of the adrenal glands. Nowadays, this chemical is often referred to in magazines as 'the stress hormone' – as though there were only *one* such hormone.

In fact, as we've already seen, there are several different hormones that are released within your body when you are stressed or anxious, but cortisol is certainly one of the most powerful. Among its effects are the following:

- It raises blood pressure.
- It increases blood glucose ('blood sugar').
- It increases the amount of acid in the stomach.
- It causes water retention.
- It depresses your immune system.
- It makes you deposit fat around your waist.
- It seems to increase your craving for high-sugar and high-fat foods – which of course aren't very good for you.

When cortisol is produced in normal amounts by your adrenal glands, it is certainly a useful hormone that helps to maintain the balance of your body. But if stress and worry make you produce too much cortisol over a long period, that can have bad effects. For instance, you may:

- develop hypertension (high blood pressure);
- get diabetes;

- develop poor resistance to infection;
- be at increased risk of a heart attack.

No wonder then that people who are badly stressed do tend to develop physical illnesses. Unfortunately, they often make things worse by opting for the wrong sort of 'stress remedy' – like alcohol, nicotine or other drugs.

These days, cortisol levels can be measured in the saliva, and that's often done in psychological experiments. However, it's not a test that your GP can carry out for you.

Overbreathing and carbon dioxide

Quite apart from the effects of stress hormones, there's something else that can affect the way you feel when you're stressed, worried or anxious: the amount of carbon dioxide in your blood.

Carbon dioxide (CO_2) is a gas that we all breathe out, in every single breath. We need a certain 'partial pressure' of it in our bloodstreams, and if we don't have enough of it, several things are likely to happen:

- We may feel peculiar, or dizzy, or a bit faint.
- We get disturbances of vision.
- We may feel panicky.
- Our faces can twitch.
- Our lips, hands and feet can start tingling.
- Our hands and feet can go into a sort of spasm.

OK, but why would the level of CO_2 in our blood go down? It's simply because we've been breathing excessively fast. This is called 'over-breathing' and it mainly happens when a person is upset or frightened. If overbreathing occurs, it washes a lot of the carbon dioxide out of bodies – and we start feeling unwell.

There's nothing imaginary about that, even though the low CO_2 level is originally caused by being het up. Simple ways of dealing with this alarming situation are explained in Chapters 4 and 9.

So is it all imaginary?

I think you can see by now that most of the symptoms associated with stress, anxiety and worry are *not* 'all in the mind'. Generally, people don't just imagine them.

In fact, many of these symptoms are directly due to the effects of the 'stress hormones': adrenaline, noradrenaline and cortisol, or to the effects of overbreathing. In this book, we'll look at good ways of combating the effects of these physiological changes, as well as ways of eliminating the *causes* of mental stress and strain.

But first, let's examine exactly what we mean by *stress*. Read on!

2

Stress

So, stress, anxiety and worry are just different aspects of the same thing: an inability of the human brain to cope with the pressures that it is being subjected to.

But what is the difference between stress, anxiety and worry? It doesn't matter very much, because really it's all a question of how the person looks at it – and what she calls it.

As we saw earlier, until relatively recently people didn't talk about 'being stressed' at all. They simply said they were feeling 'anxious' or 'worried', or perhaps that they had 'nerves'.

However, nowadays things are quite different. Out of those four terms (stress, anxiety, worry and nerves), 'stress' is by far the most common one of which men and women complain.

Indeed, I am grateful to the Google organization for letting me see a graph that shows the number of hits on 'stress', 'anxiety' and 'worry', which they recorded in the UK during 2009.

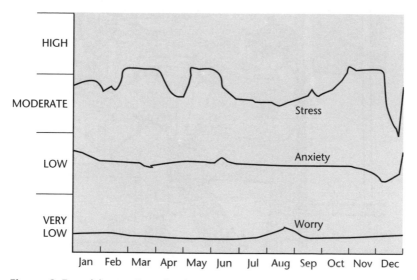

Figure 2 Enquiries to Google about stress, anxiety and worry over the course of one year (2009)

As you can see from Figure 2, which is loosely based on that graph, the word 'stress' was Googled much more often than 'anxiety' throughout the year. The number of enquiries about 'stress' shoots upwards quite markedly at certain times. But each year, it falls during the summer – perhaps when people are enjoying the sun or going on their holidays. Also, it drops off just before Christmas, when we are busy with the festive season. But it invariably shoots up in the very last days of December, possibly because of the stress of family gatherings.

So stress is now the fashionable thing to have, it seems, and a large proportion of the population talks about being 'stressed out' or 'over-stressed'. As we said, these terms are particularly common among the young, and I have often heard students say things like 'I've had three lectures today, so no wonder I'm so stressed'!

Indeed, as I was writing this chapter I spotted a headline in the *Daily Telegraph* which said: 'SEVEN OUT OF TEN HAVE SUFFERED FROM MENTAL STRESS'.

So, some 70 per cent of the population have 'suffered from stress'? Is

Figure 3 Is stress really on the increase?

there perhaps a hint of exaggeration here? You might think so ... but, really, saying that you're 'stressed' is often just today's way of saying that things aren't going very well for you at the moment.

When I was a medical student, back in the 1960s, we never saw a patient who complained of 'stress'. Indeed, the word 'stress' did not appear in our medical textbooks! I recently went through all those books, and checked the index of each volume. There was no mention of stress anywhere.

How stress has become fashionable

So how did this word become so popular? Well, it all goes back to a scientist called Hans Selye, who started doing research in the 1930s. His main interest was in investigating the way that the brains and bodies of animals and humans reacted to adverse conditions. Up until that time, the word 'stress' was mainly used by scientists when talking about such things as metal fatigue – for instance, in the wings of aeroplanes. It wasn't something you said about *people*.

The English word 'stress' actually comes from the Norman French term *destresse*, which is derived from the Latin verb *stringere* – meaning to draw out or draw tight. This is also the origin of our modern word 'distress'.

But in the 1930s, Hans Selye began to experiment with animals, such as rats, to find out the effects of subjecting them to various adverse stimuli. I'm afraid that this wasn't very nice for the poor old animals, and what he did makes pretty nasty reading these days.

Selye used various techniques on his experimental creatures – for example, flashing bright lights at them, exposing them to loud noises, giving them injections, and administering electric shocks. He soon found that these unpleasant stimuli (which he called 'stressors') produced abnormalities of behaviour, like irritability and aggression.

He eventually concluded that when exposed to stressors, most animals show a constant pattern of reactions, which he called 'the General Adaptation Syndrome'.

The so-called 'General Adaptation Syndrome'

It soon became clear that this 'General Adaptation Syndrome' also occurs in humans when they are subjected to stressful circumstances.

It's not a terribly useful term, because all it means is that there are three stages of response to stress:

1 the 'alarm' stage
2 the 'resistance' stage
3 the 'exhaustion' stage.

Let's look at each of these in detail:

1 *The 'alarm' stage.* As soon as an animal or a human being is exposed to some threat or discomfort, the body responds with what Selye called 'a state of alarm'. This initial reaction is largely caused by the involuntary release of the hormone adrenaline which, as we saw in the last chapter, is produced by your adrenal glands. (Animals have these glands too.)

The adrenaline makes you experience the 'fright, fight, flight' reaction that we described in Chapter 1. So the heart starts racing and thumping, as it tries to drive blood into the muscles in readiness for action. At the same time, one of the other stress-related hormones (cortisol) starts pumping out of the adrenals. There may also be some noradrenaline produced.

I cannot over-emphasize the fact that neither you, nor some poor old experimental animal, makes a conscious decision to enter this 'state of alarm'. It's just something that happens almost instantly – and it's almost impossible to prevent it from occurring.

2 *The 'resistance' stage.* If the stress or threat continues, the body tries to do something about it – for instance, by lashing out at the aggressor or by screaming abuse at it!

In the case of an unfortunate experimental rat, he might try to run away. A human being might do the same. Alternatively, if the threat was, say, a loud noise, a person might try to block her ears up with her hands, or perhaps turn up the volume on her iPod in order to blot out the other noise.

3 *The 'exhaustion' stage.* After the stress has gone on for a long time, there comes a point where the body just can't take any more. So, instead of fighting back, it begins to show signs of breakdown. These might include:

- trembling
- looking pale
- getting palpitations

- developing all sorts of digestive malfunctions
- feeling a 'lump' in the throat.

Obviously, this is the point when people begin to realize that they can't cope. Their symptoms get all too much, and some of them will decide to go to see a doctor.

Regrettably, other people will find different (but harmful) ways of dealing with the stress – for instance, through alcohol, nicotine or other drugs.

If this 'exhaustion' stage goes on and on, the person may start developing physical illnesses such as diabetes, hypertension (i.e. high blood pressure) or duodenal ulcers.

The Ipcress File

During the 1950s, Selye wrote a series of books and articles which suggested that the conclusions of his animal experiments could be applied to human beings. One odd result of this was that the Central Intelligence Agency (CIA) and other US government departments started to take a big interest in the effects that stress could have on soldiers and civilians – and on prisoners.

In the 1960s the word 'stress' became popularized throughout much of the world, thanks partly to a thriller novel – and the subsequent film, starring Michael Caine. The book was Len Deighton's *The Ipcress File* (1962), and the acronym 'IPCRESS' stood for:

Induction of
Psycho-neurosis by
Conditioned
REflex under
StresS

The film (1965) was particularly effective in demonstrating how exposure to stress, in the shape of flashing lights and disturbing sounds, could lead to psychological collapse. Film-goers came out of the cinema feeling mentally battered.

Regrettably, these stressful techniques were soon being used by both communist and Western intelligence agencies to induce disorientation, compliance, and even total breakdown in their prisoners.

The arrival of business and work stress

By the 1970s, the use of the word 'stress' by the public, as well as by psychologists, had become widespread. It was generally used to mean stress caused by overwork, and there was a commonly held view that tired businessmen were particularly vulnerable to it.

It was about 1975 that I first saw a patient who actually com-plained of work stress. He was an exhausted, but very aggressive, industrialist who strode into the consulting room, yelled at me that he was 'highly stressed', and demanded that I 'do something' about it. His business seemed to be collapsing round his ears and he was working 18 hours out of the 24 in a wildly unsuccessful effort to put things right. During the brief period of each day that he spent at home, he seemed to devote himself to shouting at his wife and children.

As far as I recall, the main thing that I did was to 'sign him off' work for a couple of weeks, so that he could get some rest. At that time, it would have been unthinkable to write the word 'stress' as a diagnosis on a medical certificate, and I don't remember what word or words I wrote on the little white slip of paper. Anyway, whatever I wrote, it got him a fortnight's respite from work, as a result of which things began to improve for him and his poor wife and family.

Soon after that, I started seeing quite a few teachers, who came into the surgery shaking all over and saying things like 'I just can't make it till the end of term, Doc', or perhaps 'That nativity play was really the final straw!' Very often, giving them a medical certificate saying that they had 'exhaustion' or perhaps 'anxiety' was a way of getting them a good rest, and – with a bit of luck – setting them on the road to recovery.

Incidentally, I'm not poking fun at either the businessman or the teachers. I'm simply making the point that the strains of work had got far too much for them.

How stress became a medical disorder

During the curious, self-centred and over-worked decade of the 1980s, more and more people seemed to consult their doctors because of employment-induced stress – often related to spending far too long at the workplace each day.

At about this time, GPs began to feel bold enough to write down the word 'stress' as a diagnosis on medical certificates. Rather to my surprise, the National Insurance authorities started to accept this word as a medical diagnosis. I don't remember any occasion when they contacted me and said 'What do you mean by saying that this woman has "stress"? That's not a medical disorder, you know!'

I recall that at the time I was expecting some protests from the patients' employers, especially those who were keen on getting the very last ounce of effort out of their troops. However, I was surprised to find that in general the bosses did *not* complain about a diagnosis of 'stress'. Indeed, as the years went by I realized that when an employer saw the word 'stress', or maybe the phrases 'work stress' or 'employment stress', on a certificate, he might well start thinking along the lines of 'Is this my fault?' or (perhaps more likely) 'Am I going to get sued?'

Soon, there were so many people off work because of stress that it had become a type of epidemic. Not surprisingly, we eventually started to hear about the introduction of 'stress management techniques' to indicate ways of coping with and reducing workplace stress. I'll explain these techniques in Chapter 8.

What are the symptoms of 'stress'?

So what are the main symptoms of 'stress' in human beings? Among the most common are:

- irritability
- agitation
- inability to relax
- poor judgement
- a tendency to take decisions *too fast* – in order to get out of a stressful situation
- moodiness
- nervous habits, like nail-biting or tics.

In addition, there may be physical symptoms, such as:

- aches and pains
- nausea
- bowel disturbances
- indigestion
- loss of appetite
- dizziness
- chest pain
- sleep disturbances
- sexual problems.

Also, some people become depressed when they are stressed. The subject of depression is outside the scope of this book, but it is of course perfectly understandable that if your life is full of stress, you would be more likely to develop clinical depression as well.

So there are many different symptoms of stress. Regrettably, people often try to deal with all their symptoms in entirely the wrong way. They may opt for:

- excessive drinking
- smoking
- recreational drugs like cocaine, ecstasy, mephedrone ('meow meow') or even heroin
- overuse of prescription pills, like tranquillizers or painkillers
- promiscuous sexual behaviour.

All of these 'coping mechanisms' may bring temporary relief of symptoms. However, in the long run, they are actually likely to make things *worse* rather than better.

For example, Jerry (not his real name) had been under immense stress in his job as a broadcaster. His employers were putting pressure on him to work longer hours and to travel to dangerous areas of the world. Sometimes, he was appearing before the camera when he was totally exhausted. Soon, he began to make mistakes on air. He also managed to miss a couple of plane flights, and failed to deliver a filmed report on time. Viewers complained that he seemed 'irritable' and 'rude' on the screen. At home, he had practically no time to spare for his wife, and on two occasions he found that he could not make love to her.

After a few months, Jerry developed a nagging pain in his abdomen, sensations of breathlessness, and occasional symptoms of panic. His response was to increase his cigarette consumption from five a day to fifteen, and to start having four or five large whiskies every night, without really appreciating what he was doing. He also drifted into affairs with a married 'make-up lady' and also with a young production assistant.

Not altogether surprisingly, none of this behaviour was of any real help in alleviating his stress. It wasn't until he went to a well-known private psychological health organization, where they taught him ways of managing his stress and reorganizing his life, that things began to improve for him.

Later in this book, we shall be looking at things that *you* can do to help defeat your stresses. But there are many different forms of stress, and in the next chapter we'll discuss the various types of stress-related disorders that might affect you.

3

The various types of stress

When the concept of stress first became popular, back in the latter half of the twentieth century, most people associated it with *work*. Certainly, the first patients who came to me complaining of stress were men and women who were finding the pressures of their workplace all too much for them. But as the years have gone by, more and more people have started to complain about the effects of stress in other locations. This really isn't surprising, because there are many areas of human life where stress can be intense.

However, in this chapter we'll begin with work stress, and then look at some other situations where stress can affect your life.

Work stress

Employment/work stress is extremely common, and seems to get even more prevalent when the economic climate becomes tough. Generally, what happens is that people start feeling that they just can't cope with what they're being asked to do.

They try to soldier on, but they start making mistakes at work, and this probably leads to friction with the boss, or sometimes with other employees. Before long, the person begins to develop the *physical* symptoms of stress that we've already mentioned – things like a feeling of the heart thumping in the chest, headaches, tiredness, feelings of having a lump in the throat and so on.

Let's now look at a fairly typical case of employment stress. I've changed the details so that the person won't be recognized.

Jeannie

Jeannie worked in the field of local government and was based in a large office. It was a demanding job, but she'd been doing it for years, and really enjoyed it. A pleasant woman with a happy, open face, she was about fifty when she first consulted me – about some fairly minor problem regarding the menopause. But, two years later, she came into the surgery, looking pale and shaking like a leaf.

She told me that all had been well at her office till six months previously, when a new supervisor came along. This guy was a bully. And, like a lot of bullies, he looked around till he found an easy victim. And nice, gentle Jeannie was it.

She said: 'Within a few days, he was picking on me, and making fun of me in front of all the others. He seemed to know that I wouldn't stand up to him.'

One of the worst things about this new situation was that the supervisor had the gift of getting a lot of the other office staff on his side. Before long, some of them joined in the mocking of poor Jeannie, and laughing at her mistakes – which grew increasingly frequent.

After a few weeks of this, Jeannie dreaded going to work. She'd become shaky and diffident, and she kept getting attacks of palpitations and breathlessness, plus a rumbling, uncomfortable tummy. She feared that this meant she had some serious bowel problem. Some days she would go and hide in the loo for half an hour at a time, but eventually the bully reported her to the management for this, and she was given the dreaded 'Formal Warning'.

When I saw her, she was clearly at her wits' end. She wanted me to give her a 'pill for stress', but I explained that there really wasn't any such thing. Instead, I wrote her out a certificate that stated: 'I have advised you that you should refrain from work for one month. Diagnosis: JOB STRESS.'

I then saw her at weekly intervals, and of course she reported that she felt much better while she was simply spending her time at home, doing the garden – and reading books about dealing with stress! All her bodily symptoms had disappeared.

At the end of the month's leave, she resolved to go back to work, armed with some ideas about how to deal with the supervisor. But in fact they weren't necessary.

Why not? Well, while she had been away, the bully had looked around for someone else to be cruel to. Unfortunately for him, he picked on a red-headed young Scotsman who turned out to have a core of steel. One morning, he followed the supervisor into the Gents, trapped him in a corner, and told him succinctly what was likely to happen to him if he didn't mend his ways.

Someone said that when the supervisor emerged from the loo, he was white as a sheet and sweating profusely. He then complained of pain in his chest, and took the rest of the day off.

A few days later the bully went on long-term sick leave, and never returned. Incidentally, I believe that the diagnosis on his medical certificate was 'STRESS-RELATED ILLNESS'.

And as for Jeannie, she never had any trouble with stress again.

This case history illustrates a lot of the important points about employment stress. I'd sum them up as follows:

- Very often, somebody is doing a job that is quite demanding – but with which they can cope.
- Then something happens that makes the work much more difficult to deal with.
- Instead of taking action immediately – for instance, by telling people that the new demands of the job are too great – the person tries to struggle on.
- Inevitably, he or she begins to make mistakes – at which point other people may start complaining.
- As a result, the person starts feeling friendless and alone.
- She or he takes some hasty decisions, some of which turn out to be the wrong ones.
- Because of all this stress, bodily symptoms start to surface.
- These worrying symptoms have the effect of *increasing* the person's feelings of stress – so a 'vicious circle' has been set up ...

I suppose Jeannie was lucky in that Fate stepped in, and took her tormentor out of her workplace! So her life returned to its former peaceful pattern.

But what if he *hadn't* gone? How could she have managed things?

Handling the stress

Well, there are now some well-recognized 'self-help' ways of dealing with stressful work situations. For instance:

- As soon as you realize that things are becoming stressful, *talk* to someone about what's going on. You could pick a family member or a friend, or even a helpful person at work – perhaps a union representative or maybe someone in 'human resources'. Having a chat about a difficult situation will usually ease the pressure on you. Whatever you do, don't bottle things up.
- Get out of the workplace for part of the day. The British Heart Foundation says that just popping out for a walk at lunchtime may be helpful.
- If things get bad, speak to *management*. Don't be reluctant to do this. They have a duty of care towards you. Also, these days they should be well aware that if they are at fault, they could end up being sued.
- If you feel that you can't cope, then *take time off*. Go to your doctor, and get a certificate to say that you must have time off because of

stress. Nowadays, it's most unlikely that your GP would refuse to issue one.

- Even if you're self-employed, it's better to have some time off, rather than just battling on with severe stresses.
- Don't feel bad about taking a break; no one is indispensable, whether they're a prime minister or a polecat-breeder.

Later in this book, you'll find further advice about stress management techniques, and also about psychological treatments for stress.

Family and home stress

It's a mistake, though, to think that it's only in the workplace that people get stressed. On the contrary, many bad cases of stress have their origins in the home, particularly when a number of people are living together in a cramped environment.

Many years ago, an American biologist demonstrated that when a group of rats live together in a spacious 'home', they get along just fine. But if you put them in a much smaller 'house', all hell breaks loose and they become more and more stressed.

Unfortunately, that's what often happens with human beings ...

Mike

A self-employed writer and illustrator, Mike produced humorous books for children. He worked from home in his small semi-detached house, spreading out his papers on the dining room table and scribbling away for hours at a time, and creating amusing drawings.

Unfortunately, his family life wasn't very harmonious. His wife resented the fact that he worked at home and was (as she put it) 'always under my feet'. She insisted on vacuuming all round him, and also on polishing the table while he was trying to work. As the years went by, his relationship with her grew increasingly turbulent.

They shouted at each other a lot. Also, they had five very boisterous children who came back from school mid-afternoon, and quite naturally wanted to play – noisily! And during the half-terms and holidays, they were at it all day.

So for Mike, it became more and more difficult to write and illustrate his cheerful stories in this cramped and rowdy environment. Money was tight, and he lost several book contracts because he'd been unable to finish jobs on time.

Things reached such a pitch that some days he would sit and weep over his papers while chaos reigned around him. Eventually, he talked to another self-employed writer about the problem.

This was probably the best move he could have made, because his friend suggested that he and Mike should build a spacious shed for the two of them at the bottom of the garden – a shed that was essentially a writing 'studio', with two desks, two computers, a teapot, two mugs and a kettle! Children were not allowed in it, and Mike's wife stayed well away.

This simple move virtually abolished Mike's stress. Life became even *less* stressful when his offspring grew up, and his wife went off with her accountant. But that's another story.

This story demonstrates several vital points about home stresses:

- The person feels trapped.
- There doesn't seem to be enough room at home, so clashes occur between partners/spouses.
- The presence of children seems to make any conflict worse in this scenario.
- Often, there seems to be no way out – but there is.

Handling the stress

Family and home stresses are certainly *not* easy to cope with, but here are a few tips that some of my patients have found useful:

- On days when the pressures of family life are proving too much, get out in the open air. Go for a walk – or, better still, go for a jog. Exercise releases calming agents called 'endorphins' in your brain; these are the body's natural tranquillizers.
- Avoid claustrophobic situations. No matter how much you and your family love one another, think twice before jamming them into a small room! Similarly, putting four or more family members into a little car and going on a long journey together is just *asking* for stress.
- Be particularly careful of overcrowding at Christmas. Most of us really like the idea of Yuletide family gatherings. But each year – round about 28 December – hordes of people start contacting therapists or writing to agony aunts! Why? Because they've had such a heck of a time over Christmas, with far too many adults and children jammed in close proximity to one another.
- If your children are really getting on your nerves, talk to your partner about sensible ways in which the burden of dealing with them can be fairly shared out – or, perhaps, sometimes 'farmed out' to grandparents, babysitters, child-minders or nurseries.
- If the stresses between you and your partner are great, don't hesitate

to contact a marriage guidance organization – such as Relate, or Relationships Scotland.

If, despite these commonsense moves, you are still feeling badly stressed, do seek medical advice. Later in this book, you'll find details of the types of stress treatment that are available.

Sexual and romantic stress

Love and sex are wonderful things. However, when they're not going too brilliantly, they can cause terrible stresses. That is why an appreciable number of suicides, and even murders, happen when people feel that their love-lives have become intolerable.

Violet

At the age of 25, Violet was appointed to a great job – as PA to a director of a large firm. Pretty soon, though, she fell in love with her boss, and he told her he was in love with her. They started an affair.

Almost inevitably, he was married with several children. The marriage was not terribly happy. In fact, he told Violet that soon he would leave his wife ... But the affair dragged on for almost twenty years, with Violet getting more and more stressed about where the situation was going. She kept developing minor illnesses that her GP didn't seem to be able to diagnose.

By the time she was 44, she had become jumpy, irritable and prone to bouts of bad temper. She started to make serious errors at work, and would often dissolve into tears at her desk when things weren't going well. On her forty-fifth birthday, she was fired.

Next day, her long-term lover sent her an email explaining that at last he *was* leaving his wife – but for somebody else.

The only good thing about all of this was that once he had moved out of her life, Violet found that everything was much less stressful. Six months later, she was actually in better health than she had ever been before.

Violet's tale shows some typical features of romantic/sexual stress:

- In the early stages, the person's head is 'turned' by the fact that she/he has fallen so overwhelmingly for somebody.
- However, that 'somebody' isn't really available, for whatever reason.
- But being hopelessly in love (or perhaps consumed by desire) makes it difficult to see that the other person isn't likely to turn into a permanent partner.
- Also, the two people may feel that in order to keep their affair going,

they have to resort to a lot of subterfuge – which is in itself very stressful.

Handling the stress

If your love-life is causing you immense stress, here are a few tips:

- First, consider whether you really *want* to be in this relationship; if it's causing you all this stress, is it actually worth it?
- Set yourself a time limit, by saying something like 'If this affair isn't sorted by the end of the year, I'm getting out of it'.
- Talk to your friends about it – don't bottle everything up.
- If things are bad, go to a relationship counsellor – on your own, if necessary.
- Avoid a pregnancy – this will almost certainly make everything even worse.

Post-traumatic stress disorder (PTSD)

Post-traumatic stress disorder (PTSD) isn't as common as most of the other forms of stress described in this chapter, but its effects are quite devastating.

What is it? It's a severe form of stress that occurs after a person has been exposed to some terrifying event. This event often involves someone's death, or at least a serious threat to life.

These days, most of us aren't used to such awful things taking place in front of our eyes. So, if we do see something dreadful happen, we tend to be very badly shaken up indeed. The effect on our minds can last for many years.

Here are some of the traumatic events that may produce PTSD:

- a serious road accident, in which someone is killed or maimed
- a terrorist attack
- a violent assault
- a rape
- a natural disaster, like a hurricane or an earthquake.

Typically, a person who experiences one of these things may feel OK at the time, and perhaps for a few days afterwards. But eventually, the symptoms of PTSD appear, and these may last for many years, or even – occasionally – a lifetime.

Common symptoms of PTSD are:

- bad nightmares
- 'flashbacks', in which the person re-lives the unpleasant scene

- avoidance behaviour – which means you keep away from anything or anybody that would remind you of the trauma
- displacement – which means you throw yourself obsessively into activities or hobbies that can take your mind off the trauma
- being hyper-vigilant – this means behaving as though some deadly danger is always around the corner.

Other possible features of PTSD include jumpiness, irritability, insomnia, palpitations, panic attacks, headaches, sexual problems, and depression. Those who have it often start drinking too much, or using 'recreational' drugs, in an effort to blot out what happened.

I have altered one or two details of the following story, so that the people involved will not be identified.

Some years ago, I was at a railway station in Scotland when somebody threw herself under a train. I didn't see it happen, but, as you can imagine, there was utter chaos afterwards, with people shouting or screaming or being sick. I found one of the ScotRail staff, and offered to go and certify that the victim was dead.

When I'd done that, I was taken to the station-master's office where I filled in some forms and gave my details to the British Transport Police. I talked to the train driver, who was in surprisingly good shape, perhaps because he'd been through a similar ordeal once before.

Then the staff brought in two young women, who seemed to be almost unable to speak. They had actually seen the poor woman go under the wheels, and they had virtually collapsed at the horror of the sight.

To my astonishment, they both turned out to be doctors! But they'd only just qualified, and they had never seen anything as ghastly as this. After we'd chatted for a while, and when everyone had been given mugs of strong, reviving tea, they felt a lot better.

However, I later discovered that one of them – who was only in her twenties – subsequently suffered severe nightmares and flashbacks, in which she 'saw' the incident happening again and again. She was pre-scribed tranquillizers, though they didn't help her at all. Eventually, she had to stop work for many months, until she made a gradual recovery.

What happened to this unfortunate young medic who witnessed the suicide illustrates these points:

- No matter how tough you are, the sight (or the threat) of something terrible can have severe effects on your mind.
- There's nothing to be ashamed of if this happens to you.

- If you start getting nightmares and flashbacks, you probably have PTSD.
- Tranquillizers are not the answer.

Handling the stress

What should you do if you get PTSD? Well, it's not like the other types of stress that we've mentioned so far in this chapter. It's always pretty serious, and you can't put it right simply by altering your lifestyle or by ending a hopeless relationship.

However, you should find the following strategies helpful:

- Try to get your life back into a normal routine.
- Don't work too hard.
- Give yourself plenty of time for relaxation – and do some relaxation exercises each day.
- Talk to your partner, your family, your friends and your doctor about what happened.
- Avoid drink and drugs.

Also, you really do need to seek specialist help, which means asking your doctor to refer you for psychiatric treatment. More than that, you should make sure that you go to a psychiatric department where they are *used to* dealing with post-traumatic stress disorder.

Psychological methods of treatment of PTSD and other forms of stress are described later in this book.

Combat/war stress

It's hardly surprising that people who are exposed to the awful sights and sounds of war can very often become badly stressed.

In battlefield conditions, soldiers are frequently subjected to a terrifying combination of stress-inducing factors such as noise, flashing lights, explosions and smoke, plus of course the possibility of seeing your best friend's head blown off his shoulders.

In times gone by, troops were expected to put up with such things, and just keep on fighting. The idea that a brave young chap could genuinely be incapacitated by the stress of combat was unknown. It wasn't until the American Civil War (1861–5) that doctors began to notice distinctive patterns of illness developing among men who had been in battle. In particular, there were many cases of what the military physicians called 'soldier's heart' or 'Da Costa's syndrome'.

The symptoms of 'soldier's heart' were very similar to those we often see today in badly stressed people: fast thumping in the chest (palpitations) and alarming pains located somewhere below the left nipple. As we saw in Chapter 1, these reactions are caused by the release of stress hormones such as adrenaline.

In the 1914–18 war, 'soldier's heart' was common in all the warring armies. This is scarcely surprising, as the conditions in the trenches were appallingly stressful. It has recently been estimated that as many as 80,000 British troops were affected by some form of combat stress. Apart from palpitations and chest pain, symptoms included:

- disorientation
- confusion
- shaking
- in-coordination
- staring into space ('the 1000 yard stare').

Initially, the military authorities labelled those who had these symptoms as 'cowards'. Later, it became clear that this was a genuine illness. British and American army doctors gave it a variety of names, such as 'shell shock' or 'combat fatigue'. The Germans – rather more bluntly – called it *kriegneurose* – which roughly translates into 'war neurosis'. The French termed it *psychose de guerre*, which seems somewhat over-dramatic, since there is certainly nothing psychotic about this condition.

Even during the Second World War, there was reluctance to accept that battle could actually make brave men ill. In a notorious case that occurred after the allied landings in Sicily, the US general George Patton struck a shell-shocked patient across the face, and announced that he should be shot. (He wasn't.)

Combat stress has continued to this day, and will go on occurring wherever service personnel are subjected to terrible stresses. Alas, the recent wars in the Middle East are producing their own crop of men and women who have become seriously ill because of their experiences in the battle zones.

According to the latest information, combat stress is believed to be less common in British troops than in American ones, possibly because the UK forces have had shorter tours of duty in Iraq and Afghanistan. On the other hand, it has become clear that an alarming number of UK servicemen and servicewomen have developed serious problems with alcohol, because they've turned to it as a way of dealing with the stresses of war.

Regrettably, there is still quite a stigma attached to combat stress. As I was finishing this book, an important research paper appeared in the *Journal of the Royal Society of Medicine.* Written by eight experts in military health, who are based in various NATO countries, it revealed that only a minority of service personnel who run into mental health problems will actually get professional help.

The authors say that this is partly because the stigmatization of psychological illness still creates 'barriers' to obtaining treatment. Also, many servicemen and servicewomen realize that they are not well mentally, but convince themselves that they don't really need help.

Every word of the following story is true, except that I have altered the man's surname, out of respect for his family.

Thomas

Private Thomas Hampstead was only 17 when he volunteered for the Royal West Kent Regiment in 1913. Just one month after the First World War started, the West Kents were involved in the horrors of the battle of Mons – the famous conflict in which British soldiers thought that they saw angels in the sky, fighting on their side.

Immediately before arriving in the front line, Private Hampstead and his pals had been subjected to a series of forced marches (often 25 miles at a time), which had left them exhausted, footsore and hungry. They were also desperately short of sleep.

On arrival in the trenches, Private Hampstead found that the chaos, noise, smoke and the carnage of the fighting were too much for him. Eventually, shaking and confused, he staggered away from his post and stumbled into a barn with his hands over his ears. One could hardly have had a clearer case of combat stress. Within a few hours, he was found and arrested.

Later that day, he was court-martialed. No one represented him in the makeshift military court, and he did not offer a defence. He was very rapidly found guilty of cowardice, and sentenced to death.

That evening, sentence was confirmed by the British High Command who ordered that the execution be carried out 'as publicly as possible'. So at 7.10 a.m. the next day, he was taken to a roadside in view of other troops, and shot through the heart – *pour encourager les autres* . . .

Some 86 years later, the parish council of his village, Shoreham in Kent, voted *not* to include his name on their war memorial. But in 2006, the British government issued a formal pardon to him, and to 305 other British soldiers who had been executed by their own side in 1914–18.

Private Hampstead's case history, and those of other men who were executed by their own side, show that:

- exhaustion, lack of sleep and lack of food make you more liable to combat fatigue;

- loud explosions, flashes and smoke make you prone to combat fatigue;
- a general air of chaos and confusion makes things worse;
- seeing your comrades being blown apart is a terrible strain for any human being to have to endure.

Handling the stress

If you are unlucky enough to develop combat stress, handling it is extremely difficult – but please don't use alcohol as a way of trying to deal with it.

I am *not* an expert in this field, but I would say that the sooner you can get yourself into the hands of one, the better. These days, the military authorities are much more enlightened, and therefore there are service psychiatrists who understand battle fatigue, and who know how to treat it. Above all, they know that there is nothing to be ashamed of in succumbing to this type of stress.

Regrettably, not everyone shares their view. In the summer of 2010, the noted ex-SAS author Andy McNab was reported in the press as stating that PTSD was just an excuse to quit the forces and obtain a pension. He is supposed to have said: 'It is in effect the new "back problem" – an injury that is very difficult to diagnose.' I hope he was misquoted, since this seems a strangely unsympathetic view.

Finally, please note that there is now a much-needed military charity called 'Combat Stress'. Not surprisingly, the number of service personnel who have sought its help has risen dramatically in the last few years. It can be reached on 01372 587000, or by emailing the organization (contactus@combatstress.org.uk) or through its website: <www.combat stress.org.uk>.

Performance stress ('stage fright')

Performance stress affects not only actors, but also politicians, broadcasters and musicians and (very commonly) businesspeople who have to stand up and make 'presentations' to their colleagues. Occasionally, it affects sportsmen and sportswomen.

What usually happens is that when they are about to speak or perform, they're suddenly overcome by a sense of alarm at the fact that all these people are watching them/listening to them!

Those 'stress hormones' start flooding through the bloodstream, and affecting the heart, the blood vessels, the lungs and many other parts of the body. The resultant symptoms are likely to include some of those that we've already mentioned several times in this book:

- a feeling of the heart thumping in the chest
- pallor
- breathlessness
- inability to speak properly
- trembling (which is a real problem for string and wind musicians!)
- dry mouth
- rumbling tummy, or even a sense that one is about to have a bout of diarrhoea.

In performance stress, sheer *anxiety* is more of a problem than it is in the other forms of stress that we've discussed in this chapter. Another difference is that performance problems often arise 'almost out of the blue', after only a short prior period of stress.

But when you've had 'stage fright' once, that immediately makes you stressed about appearing/performing in public again – and so a vicious circle is set up, because you keep thinking to yourself: 'Oh dear! Will it happen again next time?'

It's difficult to say *why* so many people get this kind of stress, but there are some professionals who think that it often goes back to childhood and to early experiences of being expected by a dominating parent or teacher to perform outstandingly.

In 1985, four American psychologists came up with a list of factors that seem to be present in the minds of many people who have this type of problem (see Barrell *et al.*, *Journal of Humanistic Psychology*, 25 (2), 106–22). These factors are:

- a strong need to avoid failure;
- a sense of uncertainty about 'not doing well enough';
- the idea that the audience contains significant or important people who could 'judge' you;
- a fear that those 'judges' might 'spot your failings', and be condemnatory;
- an unreasonable concern about your own appearance and behaviour in front of the 'judges'.

If they are looked at dispassionately, these fears are pretty irrational, aren't they? After all, most audiences (whether at theatres or concerts or even at business presentations) are composed of reasonable people, who wish the 'performer' well and would like him/her to succeed. But something in the thespian's/musician's brain says: 'Watch out! You may slip up, and then *they* will realize how incompetent/useless/

contemptible you are.' That is quite enough to cause copious secretion of the stress hormones, and probably overbreathing, with resultant physical symptoms.

For instance, during one difficult period of my life I felt that I had to make a number of rather demanding speeches in the debating chamber of the General Medical Council. I was speaking out against racism in medicine – of which there was a fair bit at that time.

These speeches were a terrible ordeal for me. I can recall that as the adrenaline flowed, my heart would thump, my voice would falter, and the notes I was holding in my hands would shake. At one stage, I told a friend that the stress was going to knock ten years off my life! Just a *slight* exaggeration, doctor ...

I think that eventually I overcame the stresses because of three things:

• I realized that the cause I was speaking for was a good and just one.
• I came to appreciate that most of the people who were listening to me were fair-minded and decent.
• I reached the conclusion that the very few doctors who muttered four-letter words ('What a load of ****!') during my speeches were actually pretty nasty people, whose opinion wasn't worth bothering about!

Laurence Olivier

Laurence Olivier was a wonderful actor. Yet throughout a long period of his career, he was afflicted by the most appalling stage fright.

It started suddenly in Manchester towards the end of 1964, when he was appearing in *The Master Builder* for the National Theatre Company. One night as he was about to go on stage, he felt absolutely terrified. He was convinced that he wouldn't be able to remember his lines. He staggered through the performance, though the audience seemed to him to be 'rotating anticlockwise'. However, *they* noticed nothing.

Why did it happen? He attributed it to his own guilty feelings about 'the sin of pride'. It would perhaps be more realistic to say that he was going through one of the most stress-filled periods of a turbulent life. In particular, his wife had just had a very traumatic miscarriage – though, curiously enough, it didn't occur to him that the two events might be connected.

For the next five and a half years, he had dreadful physical symptoms every time he walked out on to a stage. Though he probably sought some psychological help during that period, he claimed that 'there was no other treatment than the well-worn practice of wearing ... the terror out'. He added: 'it was in that determined spirit that I got on with the job'.

One thing that clearly did assist him was that he talked to his fellow-actors about the problem, and they did their best to help him – using such tricks as not looking him in the eye when he was speaking on stage. Anyway, for some reason his stage fright simply came to an end in 1970, while he was playing Shylock in a successful run of *The Merchant of Venice*. It never returned.

What does Laurence Olivier's case history demonstrate? I'd say that it shows these points:

- No matter how brilliant you are, you can get performance stress.
- Oddly enough, your 'audience' don't usually notice anything amiss.
- The stress may well be rooted in some irrational but deep-seated belief that you are really not *worthy* to be getting up and performing in front of all these people.
- A traumatic event in your life may spark it off.
- It helps to talk to your friends.
- Sometimes, it goes away as mysteriously as it arrived!

Handling the stress

If you get performance stress, what's the best way to deal with it? Here are some ideas:

- Don't pretend that it isn't happening – after all, it's nothing to be ashamed of.
- Talk to your partner and one or two good friends about it.
- Try to see that when you get up on your feet to make a presentation (or whatever), the idea is to *enjoy* yourself.
- Think about the fact that most, if not all, of your audience are probably on your side, and want you to do well.
- If you really have good evidence that there are some hostile people (perhaps, for example, business rivals) among your listeners, try the old speaker's trick of looking at them and imagining them naked – or even sitting on the loo!
- If the problem is occurring at work, think carefully before you disclose to *all* your colleagues that you have performance stress – sadly, you have to face the fact that one or two of them might stand to profit from this disclosure, and actually be pleased about it.

If things are really bad, it would certainly be worth consulting one of the professional advisers or therapists who are discussed later in this book.

Summing up

Whatever type of stress you're suffering from, it's important to appreciate that there's no point in just sitting back and hoping things will get better. They probably won't.

Nor is there any point in expecting that your doctor will somehow magically put things right with medication. That just isn't going to happen, particularly as there's no such thing as an 'anti-stress pill'.

However, your GP could probably help you by giving you a certificate for a short period off work, during which time you can rest and review your situation.

And 'reviewing the situation' is what you must do. If you leave things as they are, your brain and your body will simply continue to be subjected to the same old stresses that made you ill in the first place.

Therefore, you must change things. And you may well need professional help in order to do that.

4

Anxiety

Anxiety is a very common complaint. And as we've seen in earlier chapters, there is a big 'overlap' between anxiety and stress. If you have two people with the same sort of symptoms, one of them may say 'I'm stressed out' and the other might say 'I'm suffering from anxiety'.

But really, anxiety and stress are different manifestations of the same thing: a reaction of the brain to demands that it can't cope with.

What is anxiety?

If there is a distinguishing feature of anxiety, I'd say that it is this. In general, there appears to be more outpouring of the hormone adrenaline in anxiety than there is in other forms of psychological distress.

And, to re-cap, the things that may happen when your body starts pouring out adrenaline can include:

- trembling
- a feeling of the heart thumping in the chest
- fast heart rate
- pallor
- feelings of faintness
- fear of impending death.

But there are also many other possible symptoms of anxiety. For instance, you may start sweating, you could suddenly get out of breath, you might find it difficult to speak, and there could be a feeling of a lump in your throat, or even pain in the left side of your chest.

Characteristically, when the episode of anxiety has passed, all these symptoms fade away within a few minutes.

Adam
I had a pal – we'll call him Adam to protect his identity – who was a DJ and presenter on local radio in Northern Ireland. He was a 'nervy' sort of guy, but friendly and good fun. Unfortunately, he used to brood a lot about his own health, particularly when he was driving his car by himself, and therefore had time to think.

One day, while trying to navigate a busy roundabout, Adam decided that he was getting out of breath. While he was cogitating about this, he nearly steered into a lorry. That gave him quite a fright, and he gripped the wheel hard. Moments later, he started feeling pins and needles in his hands.

His interpretation of all this was that he was probably having a heart attack – though this was really quite illogical. At this point, feeling terrible, Adam stopped in a lay-by, and dialled 999 for an ambulance. He was taken to hospital, where the doctors did various tests and then told him he was OK.

Unfortunately, the next day in the broadcasting studio he suddenly experienced very similar symptoms while at the microphone, after taking a 'difficult' phone call from a rather aggressive listener. Adam was unable to continue, and someone else took over the programme for him.

That evening, he was still in a bit of a state. He went to his GP, who advised him that there was nothing physically wrong, and that he was suffering from anxiety. Adam couldn't accept this.

The next day, he had another anxiety attack while 'at the mike'. The studio seemed to him to be swimming around him, and in mid-sentence he suddenly collapsed on the floor, gasping and calling out for help.

The result of all this drama was that his employers fired him. He never worked in radio again, which was initially a very big disappointment to him.

However, one good outcome was this. Adam found himself a much less worrying job in 'admin', and then fixed up a number of sessions with a psychotherapist. She taught him how to manage his anxiety, and how to avoid regarding anxiety symptoms as indicating that something was terribly wrong with him.

These days, his life is peaceful and pretty happy. And he very rarely gets anxious.

Adam's story (in which I have changed some of his personal details as well as his name) illustrates how disabling anxiety can be. It can literally make you collapse. More often, it just makes you feel awful most of the day – and nearly every day.

Handling the anxiety

But if you deal with the anxiety correctly, you can gradually make it into a relatively unimportant thing in your life. However, you will probably need some professional advice to help you do this. For instance, it's nearly always worthwhile seeing your GP, and if at all possible you should talk to a counsellor or therapist. There's not much to be gained by trying to 'soldier on' alone.

Quite often, the best solution is to alter your lifestyle so that you're no longer subjected to the same anxiety-provoking factors. For instance, if your work makes you feel desperately anxious, then usually the best thing is to change your job.

Counselling or psychotherapy almost certainly *will* help you. But some things *won't* help, and they include:

- alcohol
- smoking
- other 'recreational' drugs
- tranquillizers.

If anxiety is getting on top of you, please don't try to solve your problems with any of the above. Instead, talk to a doctor or a good therapist about getting some treatment.

Why a little bit of anxiety can be a good thing

Rather surprisingly, a little bit of anxiety can be a good thing for some of us. Why? Because it keeps us on our toes, and prevents the famous 'couch potato syndrome'! If the entire population sat around all day, beaming happily, and never got concerned about anything, then no one would be alert to the dangers that occasionally threaten us.

And in some occupations, a little bit of anxiety is fairly essential. I'm thinking particularly of musicians and actors. They often say that if they went out to perform *without* feeling a smidgeon of anxiety, then they wouldn't be very good at their jobs.

Indeed, in a recent television discussion, a group of string and woodwind players from the Berlin Philharmonic Orchestra said that if they didn't go on to the platform with a general feeling of *angst*, their concert performances wouldn't be anything like as good.

Of course, if a performer has too much anxiety, this means trouble. It can even lead to stage fright (see Chapter 3).

In the case of sportsmen and sportswomen: they simply wouldn't produce their peak performances if they didn't have just a bit of anxiety. Remember that anxiety is largely due to adrenaline. And adrenaline speeds up the heart rate and expands the blood vessels – that is, the tubes that take blood to the muscles. So it gives you the best possible blood supply for your biceps, triceps and quadriceps, and all the other muscles that can help you win a race or score a goal.

But trouble arises when you have *too much* adrenaline and therefore too much anxiety. That's when you run into various different types of anxiety, like 'generalized anxiety disorder'.

Generalized anxiety disorder (GAD)

The phrase 'generalized anxiety disorder' (GAD) has recently become quite fashionable in the media, probably because the term has been incorporated in the international classification of psychiatric illness, the famous 'DSM-IV'.

On Google, there are over six million references to it, so people are starting to walk into GPs' surgeries and say: 'Doctor, I think I've got generalized anxiety disorder.'

I do feel that we should be a bit wary of this kind of 'label'. I recently heard of a case in which a woman who had been treated for anxiety over a period of 25 years complained that it had taken the doctors all that time to diagnose that what she *really* had was 'generalized anxiety disorder'. Looking on the bright side, she seemed to be pleased that she now had an 'official' diagnosis.

But what actually *is* GAD? Well, it simply means being anxious most of the time, without any obvious provoking factors. Thus, some people just wake up in the morning feeling anxious, and continue being anxious all day long. Even when they go to bed at night, they lie awake thinking about things that might go wrong the next day. And after they do fall asleep, they're often badly troubled by anxiety-provoking dreams.

Mary

Mary had always been a 'nervy' person. At school, she had had some difficulties in adjusting to other children, because she found them noisy and rough.

She trained to be a librarian, because she thought that the atmosphere of public libraries would be quiet and peaceful and therefore suit her. Her career went reasonably well, but she was anxious all through her working day, kept complaining of being exhausted and 'achey', and tended to get unreasonably upset if people put books back in the wrong place, or if they made too much noise in the reading room.

In her home life, Mary felt perpetually anxious about money, and permanently convinced that she was going to become broke. Friends found it awkward to go out for coffee or a meal with her, because she was always fretting about how much everything would cost.

When she was 40, the library where she worked was closed down, as a result of public spending cuts. She couldn't get another job, mainly because she interviewed so badly. Potential bosses took one look at her hyper-anxious face and then turned her down.

In some desperation, she went to her GP, who referred her to a cognitive behavioural therapy (CBT) expert. Over a period of a couple of months, he helped her to see that life really shouldn't be as anxiety-provoking as all that. Eventually, she got a nice, non-stressful job and also developed a much more easy-going and relaxed social life. [CBT is fully explained in Chapter 11.]

Mary's story demonstrates some characteristic features of generalized anxiety disorder. Those who have it tend to be:

- jumpy
- restless
- on edge
- permanently concerned that 'something may go wrong'.

They are often tired all day, and find it difficult to concentrate – because their brains are so occupied with thinking anxious thoughts. They get aching muscles, because their muscles are so tense. Also, people who have GAD tend to *look* tense most of the time, which is rather off-putting for other folk. That's one reason why those with GAD may find it difficult to make friends.

In addition, that anxiety-ridden facial expression is, alas, rather liable to deter potential romantic partners! So a substantial number of people with GAD are on their own.

Handling generalized anxiety disorder

If it's clear that you have this condition, you really do need to do something about it. If you *don't*, then it may persist for many years.

You should definitely begin by seeking advice from your GP. But please don't fall into the common trap of thinking that your doctor can produce a pill that will cure it. She can't.

Unfortunately, most people with GAD do somehow seem to get themselves on to tranquillizers before very long. But sadly, tranquillizers do *not* cure anxiety. All they can do is blot out the symptoms for a while.

You should also beware of trying to 'treat' your GAD with alcohol or cigarettes. Certainly alcohol and nicotine can have a calming effect on the brain, and so ease the symptoms of anxiety for a short time. But this calming action doesn't last very long, and soon you are likely to need *more* alcohol or *more* cigarettes in order to achieve the same result.

I would suggest the following four-point plan for handling GAD:

1 First see what your doctor says.
2 Go and talk to an experienced psychotherapist or counsellor, prefer-ably one trained in CBT (cognitive behavioural therapy).
3 Change your lifestyle, to make it less anxiety-provoking.
4 Take a look at the website of the self-help organization Anxiety UK, at <www.anxietyuk.org.uk>.

The influence of family and upbringing

In medical practice, it's very noticeable that people who are anxious, and especially those with GAD, often have anxiety-ridden parents. Again and again, when I've seen an anxious child in the surgery, she has been accompanied by a mother or a father who seems to be an absolute 'bag of nerves'. Quite often, the child seems fairly calm at that time, but the parent is getting into an awful state about nothing.

Recently I encountered a mother who was in such a tizz that she kept knocking things over on my desk, much to her daughter's embar-rassment. Later, I met a father who repeatedly got up to wash his hands in the consulting room wash basin and made his son do the same.

On another occasion, I was consulted by a dad who was so tense that he somehow managed to break the chair he was sitting on. When he got on my examination couch, he got all tangled up in the roll of paper that is supposed to go under patients' bottoms, and then kicked the examination lamp – noisily. Just imagine the effect of all this on his two children, who were sitting on the other side of the room and watching.

It is possible that there are specific genes for anxiety (and related disorders), and that therefore a 'nervy' youngster actually inherits this tendency from his or her parents.

On the other hand, I suspect that it's more often the environment in which a child is reared that is of the greatest importance in giving her/him an anxious personality. For instance, it's very difficult *not* to grow up anxious if, say, your childhood had features such as the following:

- A mother who was always miserable, and always complaining about something.
- A father who was usually cross, and kept shouting at you.
- Parents who were perpetually arguing.
- A household where there was physical violence.
- An environment in which *nothing* you did was ever right!

So if by any chance *your* daughter or son is showing significant signs of anxiety, please take a very careful look at the atmosphere in your home. Is it contributing to your child's anxiety? Is your behaviour, or your partner's, making things worse for your offspring? If so, then you owe it to the unfortunate youngster to start changing things – fast.

Regrettably, this idea seems quite extraordinary to many parents! Some of them actually regard it as an *insult* if a doctor or counsellor dares to suggest that a child's anxiety might be in any way related to his or her mother's or father's behaviour.

Useful tip: If it does seem to you that your own anxiety problems are partly related to the troubles of your childhood, try to find a counsellor who can help you explore these 'family' issues. She may well be able to help you see *why* your poor, dysfunctional parents behaved in the way they did. This can be very helpful.

Panic attacks

So what are panic attacks? Well, they're a form of episodic anxiety – in other words, they just occur from time to time. In between bouts, the person usually feels pretty much OK.

Generally speaking, each attack comes 'out of the blue'. But sometimes people keep panicking in a particular situation – for instance, in a classroom or a train carriage. This is called 'situational anxiety' (see below).

Very typically, in the early days the person doesn't *realize* that what she is experiencing is a panic attack. Instead, she thinks it's something physical, like a 'coronary' or a stroke.

According to the Royal College of Psychiatrists, one in four people who go to A&E with chest pain and a suspected coronary turn out to be having a panic attack.

Other features of panic attacks include:

- a fear that you are going crazy;
- a fear of losing control;
- breathlessness;
- a feeling that you're about to choke to death;
- light-headedness and dizziness.

Edith
Edith was a head teacher. She ruled her primary school with a rod of iron, insisting that all the staff do *exactly* as she said.

One day at morning assembly, she was reading the lesson when the words began to swim in front of her eyes. She started gasping, and then collapsed to the floor, muttering something about 'having a stroke'.

The other teachers got all the children out of the hall, and rang for an ambulance. But after two hours in A&E, the doctors told Edith – much to her indignation – that there was nothing physically wrong with her, and that it had all been a panic attack.

She returned to work the next day, loftily informing her colleagues that the hospital had found 'a minor medical problem, which would not recur'. Alas, she had another panic attack during the next Parents' Evening, and another during the annual prize-giving, and another during the Ofsted inspection.

Her response to all this was to take a year's sabbatical, and have a good rest. During this period, she met a holistic therapist who persuaded her that these genuinely *were* panic attacks, and that it was possible to 'relax her way' through them, because she wasn't going to die.

His advice was good, and Edith was eventually able to return to teaching.

How to handle a panic attack

If you seem to be having panic attacks, you need first to have a check-up from your GP in order to make sure that you really are free of a serious physical illness, and that it is just panic that is causing your symptoms.

Often, the doctor will advise you to see a therapist or counsellor, and that's generally a good path to take. Try to ensure that you get at least half a dozen sessions with her.

But during the actual panic attacks, what can you do to help yourself? Here are some useful ideas:

- When the panic attack strikes, say to yourself: 'It's just a panic attack. It's *not* going to kill me.'
- Concentrate on the fact that it *will* pass soon.
- Breathe deeply and slowly; this often has a wonderfully calming effect on all forms of anxiety, but particularly on panic attacks.
- Consider using the 'paper bag trick' (see below).

So what is the famous 'paper bag trick'? Well, many years ago scientists came up with the idea that panic attacks were often preceded by a period of *rapid breathing* (hyperventilation or overbreathing) caused by anxiety. They noted that this kind of fast, shallow breathing soon began to 'wash out' the carbon dioxide (CO_2) from the body. This idea is explained more fully back in Chapter 1.

There has recently been some controversy over the role of CO_2 in preventing panic. What is not in doubt is that when you reduce the amount of CO_2 in your bloodstream, you usually start to feel pretty awful. You may well experience fear and light-headedness, and you can get odd symptoms, including twitchiness of the cheeks and a curious 'cramping together' of your fingers.

This combination of sensations is often called 'hyperventilation syndrome' (or HVS), because the feelings are basically caused by overbreathing.

When I was a medical student, I was once asked to do this 'over-breathing routine' as an experiment in the Physiology Lab, while blood tests were done on me. As my carbon dioxide sank lower, I started to feel fairly rotten. My fingers went into the spasm that I've just described. And I'll always remember that my 'lab partner' (another young medical student) had to be taken outside – because the poor bloke was so horrified at my appearance!

Anyway, the idea of the 'paper bag trick' is to raise the CO_2 in your blood to normal levels – quickly. This can be done by simply holding a big paper bag over your mouth, and breathing in and out of it a few times. This 're-breathing' of your own air puts carbon dioxide back into your body, and so raises the level in the bloodstream. A few brief warnings though:

- Get a doctor or nurse to show you how to do the 'paper bag trick' before you attempt it for the first time.
- Don't use a plastic bag.
- Under no circumstances should you put the bag over your head!
- Only breathe in and out of the bag for a short period – a maximum of five breaths.

An alternative to the 'paper bag trick' is described in Chapter 8. Essentially, you just concentrate on taking very *long* breaths, like 'seven seconds to breathe in, and eleven seconds to breathe out'. This works well.

However, the paper bag technique is often extremely effective, not just in panic attacks, but in other types of anxiety. But be careful where you do it, as it may alarm other people. I once wanted to demonstrate it on live TV, but the producer absolutely forbade it, as he said it made him feel very nervous indeed ...

Phobias (phobic anxiety)

A phobia is an irrational but disabling fear of something, accompanied by intense symptoms of anxiety. When the person is exposed to the dreaded 'something', she will often have symptoms similar to those of a panic attack (see above).

Phobias are extremely common. Some estimates say that in the UK, there are 10 million people who have them! This sounds like an exaggeration to me, but certainly in the course of my medical career I must have seen several thousand patients who had phobias.

It's important to realize that in a medical context, the word 'phobia' does *not* mean just a simple dislike or hatred (as in 'I have a phobia about my father-in-law'). If you have a phobia, it's a 'recognized condition' (or 'illness'). You simply cannot cope with the object or situation that you're phobic about.

If you're exposed to this object/situation, your body starts pouring out adrenaline (see Chapter 1) and you immediately develop adrenaline-induced reactions, such as:

- trembling
- becoming dizzy
- looking very pale – if you're fair-skinned
- sweating
- feeling your heart thumping
- becoming breathless
- feeling tightness or even pain in your chest.

In a phobic reaction, you may even collapse. People who react in this way quite often think that they're seriously ill or dying, and may fear that the spider (or whatever the cause of the phobia is) has caused their illness in some way.

What sort of phobias are we talking about? Well, there are many dozens of different ones, as you can see by looking on the internet at the extraordinarily long lists that people have compiled there. Incidentally, don't believe in *all* of them, because some of those so-called 'phobias' are just made-up jokes.

For instance, there is *no* such medical condition as 'aibohphobia', which is alleged to be 'an irrational fear of palindromes' – that is, words that are spelt the same forwards as backwards. Look carefully at the letters of 'aibohphobia', and you'll see what I mean!

To be serious, there are about a dozen really common phobias that often cause people great distress. These are:

- acrophobia – terror of heights
- agoraphobia – terror of going outside
- ailurophobia – terror of cats
- arachnophobia – terror of spiders
- aviophobia or aerophobia – terror of flying
- claustrophobia – terror of enclosed places
- dentophobia – terror of going to the dentist
- glossophobia – terror of speaking in public
- herpetophobia – terror of snakes and other reptiles
- social phobias – these include terrors of various kinds of social activities, like talking to people, eating, drinking, touching – or even having sex.

Why do these phobias occur? And why are they so common? No one can say for certain. But they do tend to occur in people who have always been a bit anxious, and who are therefore ready to start producing a lot of adrenaline at a moment's notice. Often, there is some incident in childhood or the teenage years that involves intense fright or embarrassment.

This somehow 'imprints' itself on the brain, so that in the future the person reacts very badly when exposed to the same 'stimulus'.

Vera

Vera lived in a flat with her three children. Life was very difficult for her, because she was always short of money. Her partner often came and stayed with her, and on these occasions he always brought a lot of food and drink for the family.

But one evening, he sent her a very insulting text, breaking off their relationship. She cried all night. Next day, she found that she couldn't go out to the shops. Every time she tried to leave the block of flats, she felt quite terrified, and had to cling on to the doorpost.

For the next year, Vera was confined to the apartment block by her own fear. She knew that going outside would reduce her to a quivering jelly. In short, she had agoraphobia: fear of open spaces.

Friends and family tried to help by doing the shopping for her. Her children were very understanding, as youngsters often are in these circumstances.

Vera's GP's answer to the problem was to write out a prescription for Valium every month. Naturally, she couldn't go and collect it herself. Nor did she feel capable of visiting his surgery – and he wasn't interested in visiting *her*.

After about twelve very difficult months, her sister, Alice, came home on holiday from the USA. She had had a certain amount of agoraphobia herself in the distant past, so she grasped the situation immediately. Alice started Vera on a self-devised programme which involved the following:

- On the first day, Alice took Vera to the front door of the block of flats she lived in, and talked to her soothingly for 20 minutes.
- On the second day, she accompanied Vera to the first lamp-post along the road, stayed there while reassuring her, and then took her home.
- On the next day Alice guided her to the second lamp-post, calming her all the while.
- On the following day, she helped Vera reach the next lamp-post, and so on.

It took about three weeks before Alice could get her sister to the supermarket, but she did it. Eventually, Vera was able to go out on her own, and was effectively cured.

Vera was typical of many who have phobias. After a period of stress and trouble, she'd suddenly found herself in the grip of a severe phobic reaction that she didn't really understand.

But, thanks to the help of her shrewd, determined and loving sister, she had gradually become 'de-sensitized' to the 'Great Outdoors', and found that she could now cope with it again.

Handling phobias

If you get a phobia of any kind, try to follow the following rules:

- Don't do what so many people do – don't *avoid* the phobic object or situation. This will merely increase your anxiety about it, as time goes by.
- Try to 'expose' yourself gradually to it.
- As you do so, think about the fact that it *isn't* going to kill you or harm you, and that you will be all right.
- If at all possible, see a therapist.

Therapists have various ways of dealing with phobias. Two of the most common are 'de-sensitization' and 'implosion'.

De-sensitization is a technique that was developed by behavioural psychologists half a century ago. Essentially, it involves doing the same thing as Vera's sister Alice did: gradually exposing the person to increasing 'doses' of the phobic object or situation. Thus, a man who is terrified of spiders might at first be shown a rather indistinct picture of a spider a long way away. Then he might be shown a clearer and bigger picture. A few days later, he might watch a DVD of a spider. Later, he could view a real one, but at a range of, say, 10 metres. Over a period of weeks, he could well progress to being able to hold a spider in his hand without fear!

Implosion is a rather more dramatic technique, and I need to emphasize that no therapist would try it on anyone without getting their full permission first! The idea is that you are suddenly exposed to the full terrifying experience of your phobia, usually with the therapist by your side. This sounds pretty alarming, but the point is that you very rapidly discover that there is really nothing to fear: you do *not* die, and the world doesn't come to an end. So, for example, one woman who had a terrible phobia about snakes agreed to be taken into the Reptile House at her local zoo, and to be handed a harmless snake by the keeper. The first few minutes were very frightening for her, but the 'implosion' was successful. This woman even, at a later date, took to keeping a grass-snake in a big glass case in the garden, largely to demonstrate that she was 'cured' of her phobia.

Situational anxiety

This means exactly the same thing as phobic anxiety (see above), except that the fear is always of *situations* rather than objects. Thus a person may be terrified of being:

- in lifts;
- in trains;
- in buses;
- at business meetings;
- at parties;
- at formal gatherings – and so on.

Treatment is much the same as for other types of phobia (see above).

Separation anxiety

This is a severe fear of being separated from a particular person. For obvious reasons, it mainly occurs in children – who may become very anxious at being separated from their mothers (or occasionally fathers). In extreme cases, the child may be unable to go to school.

A similar syndrome does occasionally occur in adults, for instance when a woman who is very dependent on her husband experiences extreme anxiety symptoms if they are ever apart.

In the management of this condition, it's important not to 'give in' to it. For instance, if a small boy is desperately anxious about being apart from his mother, it won't do him any good to let him hang on to her skirts for the rest of his childhood. Parents and therapists should make every effort to 'wean' him away from his dependence on his mum, and help him realize that he doesn't need to be anxious about being away from her.

Sexual problems linked to anxiety

Several very common sexual problems are linked with anxiety. And if the anxiety can be alleviated, the sexual difficulty will often improve. There are three of these conditions:

1 *Vaginismus.* This is a condition in which a woman is very frightened of intercourse. As a result, her muscles tighten up whenever any approach is made to her vagina. Effective treatment is available from (almost exclusively female) doctors who have been trained by the Institute of Psychosexual Medicine; it involves helping the woman to relax and to diffuse her anxiety.
2 *Premature ejaculation.* This is a condition said to affect about 10 per cent of the male population. Men who have it find that intercourse is short-lived or even impossible, because they reach orgasm far too quickly. The causes of 'PE' are disputed, but anxiety and excessive adrenaline release often seem to play a part. There is a very effective behaviourist treatment, which is aimed at re-training the male, so that he approaches sex far more calmly.
3 *Erectile dysfunction.* Once known as 'impotence', this frequently encountered disorder is characterized by a man's inability to achieve an adequate erection. In younger males particularly, 'ED' is often a result of anxiety and associated excessive adrenaline production. In such cases, the problem will often disappear if the doctor or therapist can manage to lessen the young man's anxiety.

Drug treatment of anxiety

Many people who have anxiety problems have a feeling that if only they could get the right medication, everything would be OK.

Sadly, this is almost never the case. There are no drugs that will *cure* anxiety. Admittedly, there are pills – such as tranquillizers – that can make things easier for a while, by 'damping down' the symptoms of anxiety. But they can't provide a permanent solution.

Also, anti-anxiety drugs generally have the following drawbacks:

- They have side effects.
- Before long, you need to take higher doses in order to achieve the same therapeutic effect.
- You're very likely to get 'hooked' on them.
- When you try to come off them, you may develop alarming 'withdrawal symptoms', including more severe anxiety than before.

Nevertheless, I won't deny that anti-anxiety drugs can sometimes be helpful – for a short time. In particular, they can be useful if someone has to face a severe but short-lived anxiety-provoking situation.

In Chapter 7, there's a full account of all the drugs that are used to treat anxiety – and their drawbacks. But now, let's move on to a subject closely related to anxiety: worry.

5

Worry

Well, we all know what worry is, because we all experience it sometimes. My dictionary defines it as: 'a feeling of uneasiness or anxiety, especially about something uncertain or potentially dangerous'. It comes from the Old English word *wyrgan*.

Worry is that nasty, nagging feeling that comes into your mind – the feeling that something is wrong, or that something nasty may happen. Sometimes it's justified, but very often it isn't really rational at all. For instance, common examples of rather irrational worry include the following:

- Something really *bad* might happen this morning.
- I do hope my son/daughter/wife won't be run down when they're out on their own this lunchtime.
- Will there be another 9/11-style attack this afternoon?
- Is my husband seeing another woman in his lunch-break?
- Oh dear – I wonder if I'll have a heart attack this evening, like Uncle Fred did?

And even when a worry is a rational one (like 'The economy's in a mess' or 'My firm may have to close down'), many of us spend far too long in thinking about it – perhaps devoting two hours or more to pondering about something that really only deserves a couple of minutes of consideration.

A *short-lived* worry doesn't matter very much, and won't be harmful to your mental or physical health. But unfortunately, for a lot of people, worry tends to go on and on for hours or weeks or even months.

Quite a few human beings find it difficult just to cogitate about a problem for a short time – and then to quit fretting about it. Instead, they keep on turning the subject over in their minds, returning to it again and again, rehearsing what they might do to put things right, or maybe imagining future conversations, or mentally writing letters of complaint – and then doing the whole thing again and again! This is particularly common when lying in bed at night. That sort of repetitious worry is hardly ever helpful, and it's likely to cause the person a lot of distress – and insomnia.

Overlap with anxiety and stress

There's considerable 'overlap' between worry and anxiety (see Chapter 4), and people who worry a lot do tend to get very anxious. There is also quite an overlap with stress, and naturally people who are stressed tend to worry a lot.

Let me emphasize again that stress, anxiety and worry can't really be considered as separate medical conditions. They are all aspects of the same thing – namely, the reaction of the human brain to pressures that it can't easily cope with.

So it's not surprising that worry causes an outpouring of the same sort of chemicals that are produced in anxiety and in stress – chemicals such as adrenaline or cortisol. Though they aren't manufactured in the huge quantities that are suddenly churned out in, say, a panic attack, they can certainly have a bad effect on your body. That's almost certainly the reason why people who are chronic (i.e. long-term) worriers tend to get health problems like duodenal ulcers and migraines.

Normal and abnormal sources of worry

It's important to realize that worrying about some things is *normal*. For instance, in the days after the 9/11 attack, it was perfectly rational to worry that there might be another similar one. There wasn't – at least, not in New York – but it was quite reasonable to fear that another outrage might occur.

Similarly, if you find a patch of dry rot in your sitting room, then it's absolutely normal to worry for a very short time about what you've discovered. If you *didn't* worry about it at all, then you probably wouldn't do anything about it – and it might well spread throughout your home with disastrous results.

In much the same way, let's suppose you develop a possible symptom of cancer, like unexplained bleeding from the bowel or the vagina. In those circumstances, it's completely reasonable to worry about what you've noticed. In fact, it would be crazy not to. Being worried will make you go to the doctor and get something done about the problem.

It's also normal to *continue* worrying until you've managed to do something effective to sort out your problem. So, within limits, worry is OK. After all, if the human race didn't have the capacity for a *sensible* amount of worrying, we probably wouldn't have survived all these thousands of years. The ability to experience a certain amount of justifiable worry is essential for getting through life, as well as for the survival of humanity.

But there's no doubt that many of us worry far too readily, far too much, and for far too long. Very often, people waste great chunks of their lives in brooding unnecessarily about what may or may not happen.

The vicious circle of worry

Please note that worry is liable to create a 'vicious circle', as shown in Figure 4.

You worry and worry about something, and this makes your body create excessive amounts of stress hormones. Before long, these chemicals start giving you various physical symptoms. Then you notice these symptoms – and then you start to worry about the symptoms as well as the original problem. That makes you manufacture even *more* stress hormones – and so it goes on and on.

Therefore, it's important to try and *break* this vicious circle. Otherwise, you just keep making yourself feel more and more ill – and more and more worried.

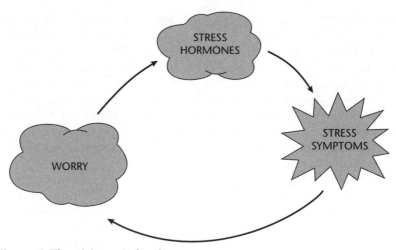

Figure 4 The vicious circle of worry

Common causes of worry

Researchers have studied the common causes of human worry. These vary quite a lot from country to country. Obviously, if you live in a part of the world where there is desperate poverty, your major worry is likely to be simply the survival of your family and yourself, and will probably include such things as the vital daily search for water and food.

But in the UK and other Western nations, worries tend to be a bit less life-and-death in their nature. However, they do vary a lot, depending on such things as what area or the country you live in, how old you are, and how well off you are.

For instance, during the most recent UK election, pollsters found that in some deprived parts of England, voters reported that their number one worry was 'immigration'. This finding would be almost incomprehensible to comfortably-off middle-class people living in affluent areas, whose major worries tended to be things like pensions, investments, house prices, and whether they could get their children into the school of their choice. A recent study suggested that the main worries of people of all classes in the UK are as they are depicted in Figure 5.

Other nations worry about different things. For instance, a recent French survey found that 54 per cent of Frenchmen and Frenchwomen

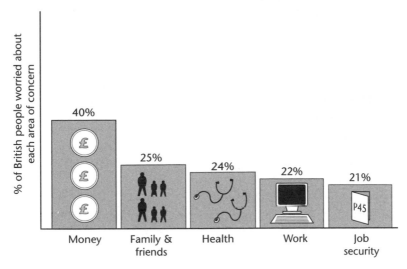

Source: Mintel 2010

Figure 5 Main sources of worry for those living in the UK

were worried about global warming. In the UK, the figure was just 40 per cent, and in the USA it was only 30 per cent.

Indeed, the USA's worries do seem to differ quite a lot from the rest of the world's. In one 2010 poll, which admittedly was not very scientifically designed, the biggest source of worry was 'the future of the US'. The next biggest was 'money and the economy', and the third biggest was worry about 'whether I will get into heaven'.

Also, what you worry about depends a lot on your age. A recent survey of teenagers in the UK found that their Number One worry was their appearance – and, in girls, specifically whether they looked fat. After that came worry about 'fitting in' with other young people. And, among teenagers in less well-off areas, subjects like drugs, smoking and bullying were very big sources of concern.

So causes of worry vary enormously. But from my own researches into what people have come into my surgery complaining about over the years (or have written to me about), I'd say that in the UK and Ireland, the things most frequently fretted about include the following:

1 Love, sex and relationships (statements from females):
- I'll never find a man.
- Does he really love me?
- I think I might be pregnant.
- The wedding arrangements are a nightmare.
- Does my husband still love me?
- Is he going to leave me?
- Should I 'give in' to the advances from Bill-at-work?
- Will Bill-at-work ever leave his wife?

2 Love, sex and relationships (statements from males):
- I'll never find a girlfriend.
- It *keeps* happening to me far too soon.
- Oh gosh, have I caught something?
- Is she pregnant?
- Do I really *want* to get married?
- I feel trapped.
- Does my wife really love me?
- Shall I invite Sheila-from-Human-Resources out for a drink?
- Is Sheila-from-Human-Resources pregnant?
- Should I leave my wife?

3 Employment:
  - I bet I'll never find a job.
  - I really *hate* this job.
  - The long hours are tiring me out.
  - My boss is awful.
  - I'm not getting paid enough.
  - I hope I don't get the sack.
  - How am I going to find another job at my age?

4 Money:
  - I'm always skint.
  - My student grant hasn't arrived.
  - On my pay, I just can't make ends meet.
  - There's never anything left over at the end of the week.
  - Our debts just keep mounting up.
  - How can I find the money for the children's clothes?
  - Where is the money for the mortgage/council tax going to come from?
  - Without an adequate pension, I really don't know what I'm going to do.

5 Confidence:
  - I always feel that I'm not good enough.
  - I fear that people don't like me.
  - I'm afraid of looking stupid.
  - I just can't assert myself.
  - I don't really seem to be good at anything.
  - My physical appearance is off-putting, particularly my face/complexion/bottom/thighs/breasts.
  - I'm hopeless.

6 Health:
  - I might get cancer.
  - I might get heart disease.
  - I might get arthritis.
  - I might get Alzheimer's.
  - My wife/husband/partner might get any of the above.

And so on. Please understand that I'm *not* poking fun at these worries. They're all very understandable – and very common. However, to brood about any of them really does you no good at all.

Why worry is mostly pointless

Many years ago, an American scholar and journalist called Thomas Kepler (1897–1963) wrote about a woman whose life was being ruined by constant worry. However, she had the insight to look carefully at the things that were making her worry, and she reached the conclusion that fretting about most of them was utterly pointless.

Her analysis of her worries has been published and re-published through several generations, and it has often been said that the statistics she produced have a lot of relevance to human beings generally. Anyway, this is what she found:

- 40 per cent of worries were about things that would never happen.
- 30 per cent of worries were about things that had *already* happened.
- 12 per cent of worries were about the opinions of other people, many of whom were motivated by insecurity or jealousy.
- 10 per cent of worries were needless concerns about health.

That makes 92 per cent of worries that were pretty useless. She estimated that only the remaining 8 per cent concerned real, relevant problems about which she needed to take some action.

What happened to this clever woman? I don't know. But there's a lesson for all of us in what she worked out. It's this: most worries aren't really worth bothering about.

Some related advice came from the enormously successful self-help 'guru' Dale Carnegie. He advised his readers that when you're beset by worry, you should just think to yourself: 'What's the *worst* that can possibly happen?' In most cases – though admittedly not all – the worst is actually something that you could cope with, if you really had to. It won't actually be World War III.

People who worry

To some extent, the human race is divided into 'worriers' and 'non-worriers'. In any crowded bus or train, you can look around and spot the people who are the excessive worriers.

They sit there with furrowed brows, peering out through the window as if expecting an accident to happen at any time. If they're talking on a mobile, they're likely to be saying something like 'It *really* looks as if it's going to rain' or 'I'm *sure* I'm going to miss my connection'. Often, their hands are clutching the arm-rest or the rail of the seat in front of them. Talk about a 'white-knuckle ride'!

Now why do so many people worry, while others always seem to be happy-go-lucky and cheerful?

It is perfectly possible that some of the tendency towards worrying is genetic in origin. Certainly, some nationalities appear to be a bit more prone to worry than others. However, I do feel that very often the tendency to keep on fretting about things is learned from one's parents. You are highly likely to grow up to be a worrier if your mum and dad were always:

- saying sentences that began with 'Oh dear ...';
- saying 'Do be careful';
- warning you that something dire might happen to you;
- saying that the weather forecast was *awful*;
- telling you that you might 'catch your death of cold';
- announcing what a dangerous place the world is.

With such an upbringing, it's really very difficult to grow up believing that 'the glass is half-full', rather than 'half-empty'! But it can be done. Not all children of parents who are worriers turn into adults who are plagued with worry. And even if you do grow up to be a worrier, it is possible to change your way of thinking, and become more laid back, particularly if you try some cognitive behavioural therapy (see below and Chapter 11).

Finally, it is worth noting that one of the UK's top experts on worry, the clinical psychologist Dr Frank Tallis, says in his excellent book *How To Stop Worrying*, that among the striking characteristics of worriers are:

- negative thinking
- an inability to take decisions.

'Negative thinking' means taking a gloomy view of everything, and particularly of your own worth. So chronic worriers are often those with low self-esteem. Therefore, psychological techniques that *improve* self-esteem will often help them.

An inability to take decisions means that it's very difficult for you to make your mind up, unless you have incontrovertible evidence that your proposed course of action is the right one. Worriers keep thinking about all the pros and cons (mainly the cons) until they get themselves into a real 'state' about what they should do.

I sometimes say to worriers that they should try to 'think like a surgeon'! You see, one almost invariable characteristic of surgeons is that they quickly sum up as much evidence as is readily available to them – and then take decisive action. They don't hang about. Not altogether surprisingly, I have hardly ever known a successful surgeon who was also a worrier!

Obsessive worrying

Some people find that they have 'obsessional' worries about one particular thing. They can't stop thinking about the subject for hours at a time.

For instance:

- A man may worry obsessively about whether he remembered to lock the front door when he went out that morning.
- A woman may obsess all day about whether her elderly mother might have fallen over and hurt herself while alone at home.
- A teenager may spend all day thinking about his or her acne, to the absolute exclusion of anything else.

If, like the above people, you find yourself spending hour after hour fretting about one particular thing, you probably have a tendency to obsessionalism (or even perhaps obsessive compulsive disorder, or OCD). If so, you'd almost certainly find it helpful to consult a psychotherapist, who would help you to alter your patterns of thinking.

If you do have OCD, that's one area where medication can be of some help. Drugs like the SSRI group of antidepressants can be useful in diminishing the amount of obsessive thinking.

Dealing with worry

Thousands and thousands of people are troubled by unnecessary worry. They spend their lives wasting time on useless thoughts, and turning things over endlessly in their minds, mostly to no purpose whatsoever. But it *is* possible to put an end to that kind of pointless thinking, as we can see from the following story.

Jonathan
Throughout his schooldays, Jonathan had been a worrier. Other kids poked fun at him, because he was always frowning and looking fearful, and saying things like 'Oooh, we might get into *trouble* ...' During his teens, he never managed to date any girls because they found him 'far too serious', and because his anxious expression and worried manner seemed to put them off.

His tendency to worry came from his parents, both of whom were nervous and jumpy. As a result, they'd brought him up to be like them: timid and fearful of life.

But at the age of 18, Jonathan decided to go into the army – much to the alarm of his mother and father, who were convinced that he'd be killed. In fact, he *was* eventually sent to a war zone, after undergoing training as a medic. Much to his own surprise, he felt able to throw himself into this new life with vigour. All his energy went into learning how to look after injured colleagues instead of worrying about himself.

By the end of his first tour of duty, he had actually saved several people's lives and been awarded a decoration. Jonathan returned to the UK as a far more confident, relaxed and mature young man. His parents were absolutely astonished at this.

So the habit of worrying *can* be defeated, particularly when a person grasps that there are much bigger issues in the world than the fairly trivial issues with which so many of us concern ourselves.

Handling worry

Good ways of dealing with worry include:

- trying to think about helping *others*, rather than brooding on your own problems;
- deciding which things are actually *worth* worrying about (very few), and which ones aren't really worth considering;
- dealing with significant worries *immediately*, rather than wasting time thinking about them over and over again.

Dr Frank Tallis says that it's vital to *define the problem.* Then, he states, you should 'brainstorm' in your own head, in order to think up about five ways of solving that problem – so as to give yourself a choice. Then you make a decision, and pick one of the solutions. This seems very good advice to me.

What about professional help? Unless you're a really obsessive worrier, it probably isn't worthwhile consulting your doctor about your 'worry habit'. But it would certainly be useful to have some sessions with a good counsellor or therapist – particularly one who uses cognitive behavioural therapy (CBT). This treatment tries to help alter the way that a person thinks. There's a full discussion of it in Chapter 11.

The therapist could also help you boost your self-esteem, which (as we've seen) is often at a low level in worriers.

In the next chapter, we move on to the many bodily symptoms that can be caused by worry, anxiety and stress.

6

Bodily symptoms

As I explained at the start of this book, there are many bodily symptoms that can be caused by stress, anxiety and worry.

These symptoms are usually quite *genuine*. As a rule, they're not imaginary or 'put on' or 'faked'. They are caused by physiological changes in the body, principally the outpouring of 'stress hormones' such as adrenaline, noradrenaline and cortisol. Sometimes, they may be due to a low level of carbon dioxide in the blood, which can occur as a result of overbreathing.

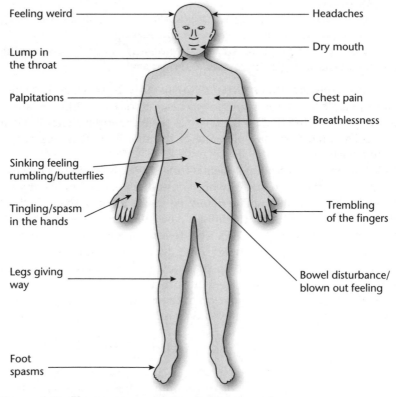

Figure 6 Bodily symptoms of stress, anxiety and worry

Now the purpose of this chapter is to list all the physical symptoms that are commonly caused by stress, anxiety and worry – symptoms that people often misinterpret as being due to something serious.

However, it's important to appreciate that *all* these symptoms can sometimes be caused by significant physical illnesses. So if you're in doubt, it's always better to check with a doctor, rather than to just assume that your symptoms must have a psychological origin.

Figure 6 shows the various bodily symptoms that you might experience, starting at the head and working downwards.

Headaches

People frequently assume that their headaches must be a result of a brain tumour, particularly if the newspapers have been full of stories about a famous person having one. In fact, I'm glad to say that brain cancer, tragic though it may be, is pretty rare. In 2009, there were only 3,700 adult deaths in the UK from this cause. I haven't seen a case in over twenty years. So you can see that the chances of your headache being caused by a brain tumour are not very high.

Other rare cases of headache include meningitis. Much more common physical reasons of this symptom include virus infections such as 'flu. And there are other very frequently encountered possibilities, like sinusitis and migraine.

However, headache is also quite commonly caused by worry and tension – particularly tension around the back of the neck and the shoulders. It seems likely that when the muscles in this area tighten up, that can create pressure on the nerves that run upwards from the neck and over the back of the skull. Result: a headache.

It's worth knowing that this particular type of 'stress headache' often responds very well to gentle muscle-relaxing massage around the shoulder-blades and the back of the neck.

Warning: But if you ever get a headache that is really severe, or persists for days, you should always see a doctor. And a headache accompanied by neck stiffness, and perhaps a rash, could be due to meningitis, and needs immediate medical assessment.

Feeling peculiar, 'weird' or dizzy

Rather similarly, people who feel a bit peculiar or dizzy (or 'swimcy' as they say in some parts of the UK) may jump to the conclusion that they have a brain tumour, or are experiencing a stroke.

But statistically it's much more likely that they are suffering from stress or anxiety, or have some minor condition, such as a viral infection. These days, young people often complain of feeling 'weird' when they are experiencing their first hangover. Most episodes of 'feeling peculiar' pass off within a few hours, especially if you lie down and rest.

Warning: If things don't get better, then seek medical advice – for instance, by ringing your doctor or NHS Direct (0845 46 47).

Also, if your 'dizziness' involves seeing the room spinning round you, that does usually indicate that you have a physical problem with your balance mechanisms, probably in the inner part of your ear. So, in this instance, see your doctor.

Dry mouth

A dry mouth is almost invariably a result of anxiety, and is caused by the action of stress chemicals on the salivary glands.

Warning: Very occasionally, a dry mouth can be caused by diabetes, or by the use of certain drugs.

Intermittent lump in the throat

A very large number of women, and a few men, experience a sensation of 'a lump in the throat' when they are tense or nervous. Characteristically, it comes and goes. Naturally, they may fear that this is a symptom of cancer. In reality, throat cancer mainly occurs in life-long smokers, in particular those aged over 60. It doesn't really produce a feeling of a lump in the throat. The main symptoms of throat cancer are hoarseness and a throaty cough.

The 'lump in the throat syndrome' is known to doctors as 'globus' (Latin for 'sphere') or 'globus hystericus'. It is caused by tightening up of the throat muscles when the person is under stress. The sensation that this tightening produces is a perfectly genuine feeling that there must be something lumpy in the throat. Fortunately, 'globus' always gets better when the person manages to relax and stop worrying.

Warning: Throat symptoms that do *not* clear up need urgent investigation by an ear, nose and throat consultant, especially if you are a smoker.

Chest pain

The alarming thing about chest pain is that it can mean you are having a heart attack (a 'coronary'). This is more likely if you're a smoker, and you're over 40. Very few heart attacks happen in young people.

However, a lot of men and women – including many in their twenties and thirties – are rushed into Accident and Emergency with *suspected* heart attacks, which turn out to be nothing of the kind, but are simply a result of stress or panic. These days, some of those 'false alarms' seem to be linked with cocaine use.

Young people are also particularly prone to the condition that used to be known as 'soldier's heart', in which there are occasional stabs of pain somewhere below the left nipple. This is often associated with palpitations (see below).

Warning: Nevertheless, you should never ignore chest pain, especially if you over 40. A severe pain in the central part of the chest could be due to a heart attack, so it needs very urgent medical assessment. If in doubt, dial 999.

Palpitations

The word 'palpitations' really means 'heartbeats that you can feel' – in other words, you are aware of the beating of your own heart. So there isn't a disease called 'palpitations', as people sometimes think. It's just a symptom.

And again and again, it is a symptom of stress and worry. Only recently, I saw an intelligent woman (a lawyer, in fact) who was convinced that her heart was beating so hard and so fast that it was actually going to burst through the front of her chest. The more she worried, the worse it got.

That kind of frightening palpitation is largely the result of an out-pouring of adrenaline, which makes the heart beat much faster and much more powerfully. So once the person calms down, the palpitation stops.

Warning: Palpitations are occasionally a sign of some problem in the electrical conduction mechanisms of the heart. For example, supra-ventricular tachycardia (SVT) is a very fast and strong 'thumping' of the heart. When Tony Blair was Prime Minister, he was taken to hospital because of an attack of it. If your doctor suspects that your palpitations could be due to this type of trouble, she will arrange an ECG test.

Other uncommon physical causes of palpitations include an overactive thyroid gland, severe anaemia, and certain drugs, including ephedrine. It's sometimes claimed that too much caffeine can cause palpitations, so it may be worth cutting down on your tea and coffee!

Breathlessness

When people suddenly get breathless, they often think that they must have something wrong with the lungs or heart. But especially in young men or women, the cause is often 'nerves'. If you get up to speak at a business meeting, and then suddenly find yourself out of breath, it's probable that this is just your body's reaction to stress.

Warning: However, shortage of breath can have serious causes, particularly in elderly or middle-aged people. Please see your doctor if you find that:

1 You cannot lie flat without becoming breathless.
2 You can't walk up a flight of stairs without becoming severely out of breath.

Tingling in the hands/spasm of the fingers

When they are het up, a lot of people get tingling in the hands. Very often, their fingers then go into a type of spasm, in which the hand forms a kind of cone.

I once knew a concert pianist who had this symptom whenever he went on to the platform to play in public, but not at other times. He was convinced that it was all due to calcium deficiency, because he had read in medical encyclopaedias that lack of that mineral can cause this symptom (yes, it's occasionally true).

However, most of the time the 'hand spasm' is actually a result of a lack of carbon dioxide in the blood, caused by overbreathing – which itself is caused by anxiety. So when the pianist managed to relax and stop overbreathing, his symptoms stopped.

Warning: Tingling in the hands and finger spasm can have other causes, like pressure on the nerves that supply the hand.

Trembling of the hands

Trembling (tremor) of the hands is exceedingly common in nervous people, and may be particularly bad in various social situations – for example, when they are called on to speak in public. The late President Kennedy had to hold his speech-notes under the lectern, so that the audience couldn't see his hands shaking.

People occasionally think that this tremor must mean they have Parkinson's disease, or some other neurological disorder. But the give-away is that the tremor only occurs when the person is under stress and knows that he or she is being observed by other people – and *never* occurs when he or she is alone.

This is really a type of 'social phobia' (please see 'Phobias' in Chapter 4). It responds well to behavioural or cognitive behavioural therapy (CBT).

Warning: Persistent tremor that continues all day, and *isn't* produced by social situations, needs evaluation by a GP, and probably also by a neurologist.

Sinking feeling in the tummy

This symptom, often referred to as 'butterflies in the tummy', is invariably due to the effect of anxiety chemicals – especially around the big nerve centre, called the 'solar plexus', which is located in the back part of your abdomen.

'Butterflies' are extremely common in cricketers who are about to go into bat, and in singers, dancers and actors who are waiting in the wings! It is virtually unknown for this symptom to be caused by anything serious.

Rumbling tummy

Although it's normal for our abdomens to rumble when we're getting hungry, quite a lot of people get *very* loud rumbling when they're in tense social situations. Naturally, this has the effect of drawing attention to them, which is usually the last thing they want!

Some people pretend it hasn't happened, while others take what is probably the wiser course – of laughing and saying something like 'Whoops – excuse my rumbling tum!' This approach has the merit of defusing the situation, so that with luck the person feels less tension.

If you get 'the dreaded rumbles' whenever you meet your boss or your mother-in-law, it's tempting to think that you must have some internal physical problem, and start filling yourself up with indigestion remedies and so on. But in fact the cause is nearly always anxiety – sometimes coupled with excessive air-swallowing, which in itself is often a result of nervousness.

Warning: Rumbling in the abdomen is scarcely ever a sign of serious disease, but can occasionally be due to intestinal obstruction, particularly when there is also severe pain in the tummy.

Abdominal distension

A feeling of being 'blown out' may also be a result of the effect of anxiety chemicals on the intestines. So people who are upset or stressed about something may complain that their tummies are 'puffy' or bloated.

Warning: It is very important to remember that in middle-aged and elderly people, a bloated feeling may actually be caused by a physical disease in the abdomen. In particular, cancer of the ovary – which is reasonably common and sometimes goes undiagnosed for quite a while – does often produce an uncomfortable, 'blown out' feeling in the lower part of the abdomen. If you're a woman over 40 and you keep getting this symptom, you should see a doctor and ask for an urgent ultrasound scan.

Bowel disturbances

Disturbances of bowel action – like diarrhoea, constipation and excessive wind – can often be due to over-activity of the nerves in the abdomen, as a result of stress.

That's probably the mechanism that causes the well-known, and very common, 'irritable bowel syndrome' (IBS). However, it's also possible that some clear-cut physical cause for IBS, such as an infection or an allergy, will some day be found.

Warning: A change of bowel habit in people aged over 40 (and particularly over 60) is quite often caused by cancer of the bowel. I have seen cases in which doctors kept insisting that a person's bowel symptoms were due to stress ('You are just blushing with your colon'), but the true diagnosis turned out to be colonic carcinoma. So if you're 40-plus and you get unexplained diarrhoea or constipation, perhaps accompanied by abdominal pain, you should insist on having a medical examination (including a 'rectal') and other tests.

Legs giving way

People who are under a lot of pressure sometimes have 'drop attacks' or 'collapses' in which their legs suddenly give way under them. I've seen a lot of this in young women who were being asked to cope with more than they could manage.

In some cases, the person actually faints, or nearly so. That's particularly common in hot weather, and in conditions of great emotional stress – like pop concerts, and the Trooping the Colour parade.

Warning: 'Drop attacks' can also have serious physical causes, like epileptic seizures, and transient ischaemic attacks (TIAs), in which there is a sudden, brief restriction of the blood supply to the brain. TIAs mainly occur in elderly people. Anyone who keeps collapsing should be seen by a GP, and probably by a neurologist as well.

Foot spasms

We've noted above that 'nervous overbreathing' can lead to spasm of the hands. The same sort of spasm can occur in the feet, and often the two are combined ('carpo-pedal spasms'). Characteristically, the toes are pulled together and flexed, while the feet are arched and turned inwards.

Warning: Very rarely, foot (and hand) spasms of this type can be a result of the physical disorder called 'tetany', in which there is often a lack of calcium in the blood.

Summing up

In this chapter, I've listed all the common symptoms caused by stress, anxiety and worry. However, as you can see, there are occasions when these symptoms are actually a result of serious physical disease. So if in doubt, please consult your doctor – and *keep on* consulting him or her until it's certain what the diagnosis is.

7

Medication *isn't* the answer

To be honest, most people who go to their GPs with stress, anxiety or worry would really like the doctor to reach for her prescription pad, and to write down the name of a tablet that will put everything right.

Alas, that's most unlikely to happen. There are no drugs that will cure stress. There are no drugs that will cure anxiety. And there are no drugs that will cure worry.

Admittedly, there are some medications that can help a bit – particularly in the short term. If you need to take these pills for a little while, just to make life more bearable, then fair enough. But you need to remember that they do not provide a *permanent* solution.

Furthermore, please remember that all drugs have side effects – and some of these unwanted effects can be serious.

Most importantly, drugs that affect the brain (and that's what all these medications do) usually have an unfortunate property called 'tachyphylaxis'. This means that the dose that helped at the start isn't so effective after a while. In other words, you may need bigger and bigger doses to achieve the same effect.

In addition, some of the drugs that are used to treat stress, anxiety and worry have pretty strong addictive qualities. That's the reason why so many people are hooked on tranquillizers.

Finally, when you try to come off some of these drugs, you may get quite severe withdrawal symptoms.

However, if you and the doctor agree that you really *do* need pharmaceutical help for a while, then that's OK. But try to use the pills for as short a time as possible.

So in this chapter, we'll look at all the medications that can be employed in anxiety, worry and stress. They fall into seven categories:

- barbiturates
- benzodiazepines
- meprobamate
- buspirone
- trifluoperazine

- beta-blockers
- antidepressants.

Let's look at them in turn.

Barbiturates

These drugs were enormously popular back in the 1960s. Fortunately, they're not often used in the UK these days, though you might be offered them in some other countries.

They include the famous phenobarbitone (or 'phenobarbital'), and they are all sedative drugs. They're called 'sedative' because their function is to damp down your brain activity. So they make you sleepy, and not very likely to care much about anything!

If fact, their effect is very like that of alcohol – and if you take a little too much of them, you pass out cold.

They are highly addictive. They're also very likely to lead to serious overdoses, or even death. At one time, quite a lot of people died because of accidental or deliberate overdosing of 'barbs'.

Barbiturates are still found in some family medicine cupboards, particularly in the homes of older people. If you find them, get rid of them. It's not worth the risk of taking them.

Benzodiazepines

In the 1960s, tranquillizers started to replace the barbiturates. The manufacturers promoted and marketed these drugs enthusiastically to doctors, suggesting that the pills would not lead to patients becoming 'hooked'. Most medics believed them. Regrettably, that claim has turned out to be quite untrue – particularly in the case of the group of drugs called 'benzodiazepines'.

Over the last 40 years or so, the world's most popular tranquillizers have been members of this group. Among the best known are:

- diazepam (formerly marketed as Valium)
- chlordiazepoxide (formerly marketed as Librium)
- lorazepam (formerly marketed as Ativan)
- oxazepam (formerly marketed as Serax).

Almost incredibly, all of the above drugs can easily be bought via the internet, without a doctor's prescription. I urge you *not* to have anything to do with this dubious trade. Apart from anything else, there is no guarantee that you are actually purchasing the drug you have ordered – the pill could contain anything.

In practice, most benzodiazepines are prescribed by GPs. To say that these drugs are still dished out on a massive scale in the treatment of anxiety and stress would be quite an understatement. I regularly get letters from people who have been on benzodiazepines for a decade or more, and who simply cannot get off them.

Yet in the UK, the authorities have been advising doctors for many years that 'benzos' should only be used for *short-term* treatment of anxiety and related disorders. Indeed, the Committee on Safety of Medicines currently (2010) says that:

- These tranquillizers should only be used for two to four weeks.
- They should only be prescribed where anxiety is 'severe, disabling, or subjecting the individual to unacceptable distress'.
- They should not be prescribed at all for *mild* anxiety.

Unfortunately, these guidelines are flouted on a massive scale. In the UK there are many people who've been on diazepam and similar drugs for far too long. And sadly, in most cases the tranquillizers aren't doing these people's problems much good. They're still pretty anxious or worried or stressed, and a lot of them are now 'hooked' on the pills. And if they try to stop, they may get frightening withdrawal symptoms.

In some cases, they're having to take more of the medication in order to achieve the same effect. This is the phenomenon of 'tachyphylaxis', referred to above.

Furthermore, quite a few people who are on 'benzos' find that the drugs slow their reaction times, which has been shown to increase the risk of road accidents.

And the thinking of those who take them may become quite muddled – particularly if they have a drink as well. I once knew a woman who took three Valium – plus a glass of dry sherry – immediately before appearing in the semi-final of *Mastermind*. Halfway through the recording, she got up from her chair, looking rather vague, and tottered off-stage. About ten minutes later, she returned somewhat woozily and sat down again. Understandably, this incident was edited out of the finished programme. She didn't win.

Meprobamate

Formerly marketed as Equanil or (in the USA) as Miltown, this used to be known as 'The Happy Pill', and for a time it was the world's most popular anti-anxiety drug.

Its chemical structure is quite different from that of the benzodiazepines, but it does basically the same job in 'damping down' your brain.

It is of some short-term use in reducing anxiety and stress, but it readily makes you addicted, and it's dangerous if an accidental or deliberate overdose is taken.

Indications are that it will probably be withdrawn from the UK market in 2011.

Buspirone

There is a relatively new tranquillizer called buspirone (marketed as Buspar), which is completely different in its chemical nature from the 'benzos'. No one seems to be very sure how it works, but it is thought to act on special receptors (serotonin receptors) in the brain.

An odd feature of this drug is that it can take up to a fortnight to exert its effect. So you can't just 'pop' a buspirone tablet immediately before you get up on stage to play Beethoven's violin concerto!

It's claimed that buspirone isn't very likely to make people become addicted, but of course that was what was said about all previous tranquillizers. Its possible side effects include nausea, dizziness, headache, and nervousness – which rather defeats the object of the exercise.

Buspirone is only recommended for short-term use.

Trifluoperazine

Trifluoperazine (marketed as Stelazine) is a major tranquillizer, only used for very severe anxiety, and also for psychotic illnesses. Side effects include serious neurological disorders and blood problems.

This drug is extremely powerful, and its use in cases of anxiety should be limited to very short-term treatment – for instance, simply to cover an emergency.

Beta-blockers

Beta-blockers are *not* tranquillizers, but they are used quite frequently to treat certain manifestations of anxiety or stress, particularly trembling of the hands.

What are they? They're a group of drugs that were invented by British scientist Sir James Black, who wanted to find agents that could block some of the actions of adrenaline. This effect makes them very useful in the treatment of conditions like high blood pressure and angina.

Their ability to block adrenaline does also make them pretty effective in reducing or abolishing some of the symptoms of anxiety and stress, particularly tremor and palpitations. Indeed, they are so effective in combating shaky hands that they're quite widely used by musicians, and also by sportsmen and sportswomen.

Among the sports where they have been employed in order to reduce anxiety-induced hand tremor are snooker, billiards, rifle-shooting and, in recent years (according to Tiger Woods), golf.

The professional snooker authorities have been testing for illegal beta-blocker use since the 1980s. Some players have claimed that they ought to be allowed to take beta-blockers, provided a doctor has prescribed the drugs for a genuine medical condition. However, the World Confederation of Billiard Sports (WCBS) has now ruled that beta-blockers are absolutely banned, and that no application for 'therapeutic use exemption' will be accepted.

But in everyday life, there is no reason why you shouldn't try beta-blockers if your doctor agrees – and if you have no medical contra-indications. The ones that are most often used in order to abolish tremor or palpitations are propranolol (marketed as Inderal or Half-Inderal) and oxprenolol (marketed as Trasicor and Slow-Trasicor).

Warning: Please note that propranolol and other beta-blockers must not be used by people who have asthma, heart block and certain other medical conditions. Disregarding this rule can have very serious consequences.

Side effects of propranolol and related beta-blockers can include tummy upsets, excessively slow pulse, fatigue, sleep problems, sexual dysfunction, heart failure and many others.

Antidepressants

Although depression is outside the scope of this book, a number of drugs that are used to treat depressive illness do also have a UK licence for use in anxiety.

To be frank, in the last few years considerable doubts have been cast on the effectiveness of these drugs in helping people with depression. And I cannot say that the evidence for their value in treating *anxiety* is exactly overwhelming.

Nevertheless, the following antidepressants are sometimes used in the treatment of anxiety, and some of them are prescribed for panic disorders or phobias, or for post-traumatic stress:

- venlafaxine (Efexor XL)
- citalopram (Cipramil)
- escitalopram (Cipralex)
- paroxetine (Seroxat)
- sertraline (Lustral)
- dosulepin (Prothiaden)
- trazodone (Molipaxin)
- amitriptyline (combined with perphenazine in Triptafen)
- flupentixol (Fluanxol).

I cannot over-emphasize the fact that all these antidepressants are powerful drugs, and associated with a lot of potential side effects – which vary a lot from brand to brand.

I can't honestly say that if I were suffering from an anxiety-related disorder, I would really want to take any of them.

Summing up

So tranquillizers such as diazepam can be of some use in the initial treatment of anxiety, panic and stress – provided you don't stay on them for long. It is vital that you don't let yourself get 'hooked'.

Also, the beta-blocker group can be of value in reducing certain anxiety symptoms, particularly shaky hands.

However, the true answer to stress, anxiety and worry isn't to be found in drugs. What you really need is to do two things:

1 Deal with the _causes_ of your problems.
2 Alter the way in which you handle your difficulties.

In the rest of this book we'll be looking at the methods by which you can achieve these two objectives.

8

Lifestyle changes

We've seen that medication is unlikely to give you more than a temporary respite from stress, anxiety and worry. And so, in order to defeat these conditions, you need to do two things:

1 Alter your life so as to *diminish* the stress, anxiety and worry that you're exposed to.
2 *Change* the way in which you handle these 'stressors' when you're faced with them.

In this chapter, we'll look at ways in which you can alter your life. And in the next chapter, we'll be examining techniques for changing the way in which you handle those 'stressors'.

Altering your life

People often say to me: 'Oh, but I couldn't possibly change my life!' Then they find out that they can.

So how can you reduce the problems in your life? Well, the first thing is to accept that you *can* make changes. Then you can set about starting to make them. Very often, just a simple move can alter things dramatically. For instance, I knew a businessman who found travelling enormously stressful. Unfortunately, he had to journey abroad a great deal in his work, taking along his wife, who was also his business partner.

The big problem was that as he went through check-in and security and customs, he got himself into a terrible state about whether he still had the tickets and passports and boarding cards and other documentation. By the time the two of them had arrived at their destination, he was a bag of nerves.

So how could he modify things? A psychologist friend suggested a brilliantly straightforward answer. He said: 'Just give all the paperwork to your wife.'

And that was all there was to it for this man! His wife, who was a very calm and capable woman, was perfectly happy to take on the job of looking after tickets, boarding passes and all the other travel documents for the two of them. She put them all in a small plastic folder, and kept it in an outer compartment of her handbag.

So, this ridiculously simple piece of advice immediately removed nearly all the stress and worry of travel from the unfortunate business-man's shoulders.

In the same way, *you* need to look hard at all the things that are causing you stress and strain – and see what you can do to modify them. First, let's consider problems relating to your job.

What can you do about your stressful job?

If your job is very stressful, you should examine the aspects of it that are causing you real trouble, and try to find a way of dealing with them.

Let's look at a few possibilities:

- *You've always hated your job and you always will.* Answer: If things are really as bad as that, then for the sake of your health and sanity you ought to get out as soon as possible! There are other jobs, you know. But even being unemployed is better than doing something that is probably going to make you ill.
- *You hate the commute to work.* Answer: Then move to somewhere nearer to your workplace. Or ask the firm for a transfer to some-where near your home town. Or, if you can, switch to working from home. If none of these solutions is possible, then why not just get an earlier train, so that your journey is less crowded? Another pos-sibility is to use the time on the train to work or study – if there's room. And another very good way to reduce commuting stress is to get yourself an MP3 player or an iPod, and play yourself soothing music all the way to work.
- *There's someone at work who is bullying you or giving you lots of hassle.* Answer: Keep a written record of all instances of bullying. Contact your union, if you have one. Go to Human Resources (or whoever's in charge) and complain. If there's no one at work who will listen, then consult a solicitor.
- *Somebody at work is sexually harassing you.* Answer: As for the point above and, if necessary, contact the police.
- *Your chair or desk or computer are causing you pain and discomfort.* Answer: These days, no one should be expected to put up with that kind of thing. So insist on a change. Your employer should be aware that if his furniture or equipment is making you ill, he could be sued.
- *The hours are far too long, and you're always shattered.* Answer:

Nowadays, no one should be doing a job that leaves them utterly exhausted. You have three main choices, which are: (1) ask for a reduction in hours; (2) go part-time; or (3) leave the job.

Later in this chapter, we'll look at ways of *organizing* work so that it's less of a stressor.

What can you do about your stressful love-life?

In much the same way, if your love-life is so awful that it's making you ill with stress or worry, then *do* something about it. For instance:

- *Your partner is consistently unfaithful, and is causing you great unhappiness.* Answer: Ditch this person. There are literally tens of millions of more suitable people in the world. Why stay with one who causes you such grief?
- *Your partner is violent to you.* Answer: Get out of this relationship. Contact the police, and also one of the organizations for battered spouses/partners, like Women's Aid (<www.womensaid.org.uk>).
- *You're hopelessly confused because you're torn between two partners.* Answer: You have to bail out of this situation. There is virtually never a 'three-way' solution, in which a person manages to have a happy, long-term, loving relationship with two other people. Very often, the best thing to do is to decide that you're going to go away somewhere, and not see *either* of them again for a year. By the end of that time, things will probably look very different.

What can you do about your stressful family life?

Well, whatever is wrong with the family structure, it can be fixed – if you're determined enough to put things right. For example:

- *You and your partner never get any time together.* Answer: Be firm. Tell your partner that these days it's almost impossible for a marriage, or a relationship, to survive unless the couple have a fair amount of time on their own. Agree on a fixed, minimum chunk of time that the two of you will spend together (perhaps two hours a day, five days a week). Then move heaven and earth to ensure that you get it. Obviously if you or your partner have a job that requires you to go away for lengthy periods – perhaps you are in the services – this is not always possible to alter.
- *Your in-laws are awful.* Answer: Again, be firm. You don't have to put up with these people for unreasonable periods of time. Make an

agreement with your partner that you will only see the in-laws for a strictly limited amount of time. Depending on what you can stand, this could be for three hours a week – or three hours a year!

- *Your children are terribly demanding, and are making your life a misery.* Answer: You must take steps to get them under reasonable control – and you may need the help of a counsellor or therapist to do it. Remember that you don't have to spend every waking hour with your children. There are such people as babysitters and child-minders, and also grandparents.
- *Your partner and you row incessantly.* Answer: This is bad – especially for the health of both of you. Constant rowing means that the relationship is in trouble. Go and see someone at Relate or (if you're north of the border) Relationships Scotland.

Reorganizing your life and work

Now, it's often quite possible to reorganize both your work *and* your home life so that it's less of a cause of stress. May I give you an example.

A couple of years ago, a psychotherapist went to see her GP about a sore throat. While she was in the consulting room, she noticed that the doctor seemed to be exceedingly stressed!

There were piles of documents all over her desk. The papers were mixed up with all sorts of small bits of medical equipment – like knee-jerk hammers and throat torches. It was obvious that the doctor couldn't find anything without a hunt for it.

While she was trying to hold the consultation, phone calls kept coming in. Sometimes it was just a receptionist, wanting to know if the GP was ready for her cup of tea. Other times, it was a patient calling in for advice about an emergency.

Every couple of minutes, practice staff kept walking in with messages for this doctor. There were also text messages appearing on the screen. The GP was trying to read them, at the same time as doing everything else, but she was having serious problems with working the computer, and it seemed that whenever she hit a key, the screen went blank.

Very sympathetically, the psychotherapist leaned forward and said: 'Please let's forget about my sore throat. Instead, let me help sort out how you could organize your work.'

Rather surprisingly, the GP agreed. Within ten minutes, the psycho-therapist had shown her how to organize herself far more efficiently. In summary, she advised her to:

- clear her desk of everything but a pen and a pad of paper;

- order the staff not to put through any phone calls while she was with a patient;
- instruct them that they mustn't wander in while she was consulting;
- tell people not to send her text messages during a surgery;
- enrol herself on a simple computer course!

Almost inevitably, these few simple pieces of advice had quite a dramatic effect on the GP's life. She became far less stressed, and she also became far better at listening to her patients and helping them.

In a rather similar way, the same psychotherapist was able to assist one of her own clients who was a desperately hassled mother, trying to work from home, but spending much of her day in chaotic attempts to clear up after her selfish partner and her four demanding children.

Essentially, the psychotherapist put this poor mother on a 'time management scheme' (see below), and this helped her to bring some order into her life. As a result, she became much less anxious and stressed.

You could achieve the same thing ... Yes, you really could!

Time management

A really good way of minimizing the stresses and anxieties in your life is to opt for 'time management'.

What is it? Well, it's a way of planning your day, or your week, so that you know roughly what you're going to have to do. Most importantly, you shouldn't get involved with doing other things *except* in the case of an emergency, or for some other really good reason.

Other essentials of good time management include:

- only doing one task at a time;
- not trying to 'jam in' other things in the minute or two between tasks;
- allowing enough time for the unexpected;
- being prepared to say 'No' to people who want you to do things that aren't in your schedule;
- avoiding putting things off – generally, this only increases stress and worry;
- dealing with letters or emails only *once*, which means that you shouldn't put them aside, brood over them, and re-read them five times – make your motto 'HOO', which means 'Handle Only Once'!

It's often a good idea, particularly when you're under a lot of pressure, to make yourself a daily 'Time Management Chart'. The idea is that you

TIME:	MY PLAN:	WHAT ACTUALLY HAPPENED:
7 am – 8	GET UP GET CHILDREN FED AND DRESSED.	Overslept, as exhausted. Caught up!
8 am – 9	DRIVE KIDS TO SCHOOL.	Traffic jam. Late. Must allow more time.
9 am – 10	RETURN HOME. CHECK TODAY'S EMAILS & REPLY.	Delayed again! OK.
10 am – 11	WRITE ARTICLE FOR 'EXPRESS'.	Wrote half of it.
11 am – Noon	WORK OUT AT GYM.	Sister rang, so never got there. Shouldn't have picked up the phone.
Noon – 1 pm	RING AGENT TO DISCUSS MY NEW BOOK.	OK.
1 pm – 2	QUICK LUNCH WITH FRIEND.	Friend in tears over husband, so lunch lasted two hours!
2 pm – 3	RING 'MAIL' TO OFFER THEM AN ARTICLE.	Never got time to do this! Ought to have stopped friend sooner.
3 pm – 4	PICK UP CHILDREN. GIVE THEM TEA.	OK, but running late.
4 pm – 5	HELP KIDS WITH HOMEWORK.	OK.
5 pm – 6	READ TO SON. PLAY GAMES.	OK.
6 pm – 7	PREPARE SUPPER.	OK, but daughter was sick.
7 pm – 8	GET KIDS TO BED.	OK, but they kept demanding more stories.
8 pm onwards	DO MY ACCOUNTS AND RING MUM.	No. Worn out. Fell asleep in front of TV.

Figure 7 Time management chart

draw this up in the morning (or the night before), plotting out what you're going to do, hour by hour. At the end of each day, you can write in what you actually *did*! You can see what I mean by looking at Figure 7, which represents a day in the life of a busy mother who also works as a writer and journalist.

You don't have to follow your chart obsessively, and there will be times when outside events force you to modify your plans. But it does give you a structure for the day, and you'll find that by bedtime you don't have so many uncompleted jobs to worry about. That in itself will reduce stress and anxiety.

Prioritizing

This is another useful stress control technique, for use in work and in life generally. If you seem to be overwhelmed by all kinds of different 'stressors', just sit down for a moment and reflect.

Have you been running around like the proverbial headless chicken, trying to sort loads of things out in a chaotic way? Then take a pen and paper, and write down what you think are the real *priority* things that you need to handle.

For instance, a teacher called Brian was having a tough time on a Sunday night. His wife had just slammed the front door in a rage and gone off to her mother's for the evening. Upstairs, their baby was crying. Downstairs, their three-year-old was yelling that his finger was hurting, and that he had tipped the remains of his supper on the floor. On the dining room table was a pile of school essays that *had* to be marked by the following morning. And in the sitting room, the television had just packed up. Meanwhile, in the bathroom the tap had got jammed in the 'closed' position, so that there was no hot water upstairs. On the mobile phone, there were several new text messages from an ex-girlfriend who wanted to get in touch again. Quite a lot of stress there!

A chaotically organized person would have galloped round the house, getting more and more stressed, and trying – in between tasks – to mark the odd essay.

However, Brian's approach was to prioritize. What actually *needed* doing? In his view, the important things were:

1 Making sure the baby was all right. (She was.)
2 Ensuring that the three-year-old was OK. (He was; and once he was tucked up in bed, his finger stopped hurting.)
3 Sitting down calmly in a quiet room and getting the essays marked for the morning.

Everything else, Brian reasoned, could wait. His wife would probably come home by midnight. He could leave clearing up the wreckage of the toddler's supper till about 11 p.m. The broken television could wait until tomorrow. And in the morning, he could ask a plumber to come and fix the bathroom tap – thereby avoiding creating a flood that night! As for the texts from the ex-girlfriend, he could simply ignore them.

Peacefully, he settled down to an evening's marking, having first switched on Radio 3 to get some nice, soothing music.

And so, they all lived happily ever after ...

In the next chapter I'll explain how you can change the way in which you deal with 'stressors', so that your body and mind remain calm.

9

Training your mind and body to cope

In the previous chapter, we looked at ways of rearranging our lifestyles so that we are exposed to a minimum of stress, worry and anxiety.

However, the fact is that whatever we do, all of us will run into quite 'difficult' situations, virtually every day of our lives. So it's inevitable that we will continue to encounter various 'stressors', for as long as we live.

But happily, there are ways of re-training the mind and body so that we cope much better with whatever fate throws at us. In fact, it is possible to be a lot calmer – and a lot happier too. It's also well within our powers to get rid of the *physical* symptoms of stress, anxiety and worry.

Re-training your mind

If you suffer from stress or anxiety or worry, you really need to 're-train' your mind in order to deal with these things. This is the basis of 'cognitive behavioural therapy' (CBT), which has achieved such successes in recent years (see Chapters 10 and 11).

But altering your mental processes won't just happen magically. You have to make a real effort to alter the way you think about the 'slings and arrows' of life. Let's take an example:

A guy called Henry is setting off for work in the morning. It's icy, and as he walks down his front path he slips and twists his ankle. When he gets to his front gate, he finds that a vandal has pulled it off its hinges. He steps outside and puts both feet in a pile of dog poo. He scrapes the mess off as best he can, and then looks up to see that his bus to the station is pulling away. So he's going to be late for work.

Now there are two ways in which a person can react to all these 'stressors'. Here's the first way:

- When Henry twists his ankle, he can swear loudly, and feel that once again Life is being unfair to him.
- When he discovers the broken front gate, he can erupt with fury.
- When he treads in the dog poo, he can start leaping up and down,

and deciding that it must be the fault of that *stupid* dog-owner next door.
- When he misses his bus, he can throw his hat on the pavement – and then jump on it.

Now here's the second way:

- Henry checks his ankle, finds that he can walk without a limp, and says to himself: 'Thank goodness it's not broken'.
- He looks at the gate, reflects that it's pretty old anyway, and decides that he can easily fix it that evening – or get a better gate.
- Seeing that his shoes are pretty messy, he goes back into the garden and leaves them under a bush; then he pops back into the house and gets another pair.
- When he sees the bus disappearing over the horizon, he laughs; then he enjoys a brisk walk to the station, where he has a nice cup of coffee while waiting for the next train.

Now, which Henry do you think is coping better with the problems of life? Obviously, it's the second one, isn't it?

But the fact is that you can *train* yourself to think like 'the second Henry' – provided you make a real effort to do this. So, when something goes wrong, you should immediately concentrate on the *best* aspect of what has occurred. Often this involves coming up with thoughts like: 'Well, at least it's not as bad as if 'x' or 'y' had happened ...'

Initially, this kind of 'Always look on the bright side' approach may sound a bit over the top, like something from the Monty Python film *Life of Brian* or *Pollyanna*. If you're not American, you may not know that Pollyanna is a lovable, insanely optimistic character in an extraordinarily successful series of US books, published between 1913 and 1997; her determination to see everything in the best possible light led to the series being called 'The Glad Books'.

But in fact recent research has shown that if – like Pollyanna – you can keep thinking positively about things that happen to you, this has a beneficial effect on your entire state of mind. You become calmer, and you get better at coping with problems and crises.

And, very importantly, this alteration in your thinking soon starts to alter the reactions of your body.

Modifying your body's responses

Back at the beginning of this book, we discussed the fact that many physical symptoms of stress, anxiety and worry, ranging from palpitations to trembling, are mainly caused by adrenaline and other 'stress chemicals'. You'll probably remember that other bodily symptoms are caused by 'overbreathing' (hyperventilation), which washes out the carbon dioxide (CO_2) in your bloodstream.

I said in Chapter 1 that all these distressing symptoms aren't really under your conscious control. However, the good news is that if you use certain simple procedures to calm your brain, then it *ceases* sending out alarm signals to various parts of your body.

In particular, a calmed brain will:

- stop telling your adrenal glands to pour out 'stress hormones' such as adrenaline, noradrenaline and cortisol;
- stop telling your lungs to breathe faster, so that you lose CO_2.

Now let's look at some of the simple techniques that can create calmness in your brain, and peace in your body.

Breathing techniques

A very simple thing that you can is to re-train your breathing habits. Many people, particularly those who are under pressure, breathe too fast – and too shallowly.

As mentioned above, this washes a lot of CO_2 out of the body, and makes you feel unwell. Recent medical research has suggested that there may be a lot more to it than that, but pretty well all experts agree that if you make yourself breathe properly, you will feel better. Here's what you do:

- Several times a day, make a conscious effort to spend the next few minutes concentrating on your breathing.
- You can carry this out wherever you are – on a bus, in a car, sitting in a chair, or lying in bed.
- Tell yourself that you're going to take much *longer* breaths.
- Breathe in slowly, counting up to seven as you do so.
- Then breathe out even more slowly, this time counting up to 11.
- Not surprisingly, this is called the '7/11 method'.
- To start with, just keep it up for five minutes.
- You'll find that you only take about 20 breaths during that time.
- Later on, you can make the sessions far longer.
- Eventually, you may be able to do this kind of breathing during quite long periods of the day.
- Note how calm this makes you feel.

- Also note that it has a beneficial effect on bodily symptoms that are linked with stress and anxiety.

Incidentally, this is a very good way of dealing with a panic attack.

Relaxation techniques

Apart from deep breathing, there are various useful techniques for relaxing your mind and body. For instance:

- *Listen to relaxation tapes and CDs.* These days, you can buy these very cheaply, and listen to them on your own headphones. It's good to do this lying flat on a bed, or sitting in a comfortable chair. But you can also listen to them in a busy train or a crowded bus, and 'de-contract' yourself as you travel. (But you'd better not use them when you're driving, in case you fall asleep.) These tapes and CDs employ various methods to relax you, like playing soothing noises – such as the sound of gentle waves. They're always 'narrated' by someone with a really calming, reassuring voice. They will usually encourage you to breathe properly. And they may well teach you the 'muscle de-contracting' method (see below).
- *Use muscle de-contraction.* This is a very useful technique in which you contract various muscle groups in the body – and then relax them and see how nice and laid-back it feels! You really need to learn the method from a relaxation tape/CD or a therapist, but essentially what you do is to lie down in a pleasant quiet room and, after a minute or so, curl your toes up really hard for ten seconds or so – and then let them go completely slack. When you've enjoyed the pleasant feeling this produces, you do exactly the same thing with the muscles in your feet. After that, you work upwards through all the main muscle groups in your body, which should take about 20–25 minutes. At the end of it all, you should feel wonderfully relaxed. It's a good idea to repeat the procedure at least once a day.
- *Employ 'visualization'.* The idea of this is that you lie or sit somewhere quiet with your eyes shut, and then imagine yourself going to a very safe, secure, stress-free environment. It's probably best to get a therapist or counsellor to teach you how to do this, but you can learn it without professional help. Begin by deciding what the nicest and safest location in the world would be for you. It could be a cosy room in a country cottage, or perhaps a sunlit field by a tranquil river. Then say to yourself: 'I am going to my favourite place ...'

Next, imagine yourself making a short, pleasant, easy journey there. Some people interpret this as walking up or down a flight of stairs, or making a brief journey in a lift. Whatever you choose, you imagine yourself arriving at this lovely place, and then lying back and really enjoying the delights of sheer relaxation. Ah, bliss! Believe me, it really does work.

Stretching

Curiously enough, simple stretching exercises are very useful in helping a person who is under pressure. You've seen cats – or indeed, big cats at the zoo – stretch their muscles and yawn when they want to let everything go.

Well, the principle is the same for human beings. When the going gets tough, it's a good idea to take time out somewhere – preferably somewhere quiet – and then spend ten minutes stretching out your arms, legs, shoulders, back and neck. For some reason, this works best if you begin by clenching your fists.

If you do it right, you'll soon find yourself yawning, very like a large lion who's just given up for the day.

Exercise

All experts agree that exercise is very good indeed for people who are weighed down by stress, worry and anxiety. There are several possible reasons for this, including the fact that exercise has a remarkable capacity for 'burning up' those stress chemicals – like adrenaline, for example. This is not surprising, when you consider that one of the major functions of adrenaline is to prepare the body for running or fighting.

Also, there is the important point that exercise makes the brain release chemicals called 'endorphins'. As we noted earlier, these are the body's natural tranquillizers, and they seem to have an extraordinarily soothing effect on people. Research done in 2008, using the form of brain imaging called 'Positron Emission Tomography' (PET), suggests that when we exercise, endorphins attach themselves to the emotional centres of the brain, and calm everything down.

All distance runners are aware of the effects of endorphins, because they know that when they've been going for about twenty minutes, a pleasant kind of peace seems to descend on the brain. In the 1970s, this used to be called 'athlete's euphoria' or 'runner's high'. Today, some GPs actually hand their patients a piece of paper marked:

PRESCRIPTION:
Exercise five times per week

Mind you, I don't know how many of the patients pay any attention to this particular prescription ...

Sport – and dancing

Because exercise has a good effect on stress, worry and anxiety, it's obvious that playing sport does too. The main exceptions to this are those sporting activities that involve virtually no physical effort – such as darts, snooker, billiards, pool and chess.

In addition, you might want to avoid sports that you know will actually *increase* your stress. Personally, I gave up golf after I took eight shots to hole out at the Par Four seventh. Then I gave up golf *again* the following week – and the week after that ...

But most sports are beneficial in relieving anxiety, stress and worry. That goes for dancing too, because it's a fairly vigorous form of exercise. I've known stressed patients make themselves feel a lot better by simply turning on the radio and dancing in front of it for half an hour a day.

Meditation

There's no question that meditation can be good for relieving stress, worry and anxiety. But I don't mean sitting around and brooding! It has to be *real* meditation, and you do need to be taught how to do it by someone who is skilled in the practice.

There are literally hundreds of different types of meditation, and I recommend that you find a teacher from your local *Yellow Pages*, or via the internet. Incidentally, many people have the idea that meditation *must* mean 'Transcendental Meditation' (TM), which has been well known ever since the Beatles took it up nearly half a century ago. You may perhaps like to note that 'TM' is actually a trade-marked term, associated with the group known as the Natural Law Party. There are many alternatives available.

Meditation is a soothing process, in which you sit comfortably, and focus all your attention on one object or perhaps one phrase. It's important that you practise it in a quiet place, like a room where you won't be disturbed or somewhere peaceful outdoors. You need to do it regularly – probably once or twice a day. Turn off your phone before you start!

Whoever teaches you will show you how to achieve complete relaxation through meditation. With luck, your stresses and strains will gradually melt away.

Yoga

If you type the words 'yoga for beginners' into Google, you'll find yourself with a choice of nearly a million websites. This does show you how fantastically popular yoga is these days.

It doesn't appeal to everybody, but a lot of people do find that it is very effective in relieving their stresses and strains. It relaxes your muscles and your joints and, if done properly, relaxes your mind too.

There are many different types of yoga, but in the UK and other Western countries, the word 'yoga' most often means the kind called 'hatha yoga'. In Sanskrit, the expression '*ha-tha*' means 'sun and moon', but many scholars translate the term as meaning 'strong' or 'powerful'.

Hatha yoga involves learning various *asanas* (postures and movements), as well as learning about correct breathing and practising meditation. Some *asanas* are supposed to be particularly good for defeating worry, and combating panic attacks.

Certainly, I have encountered quite a few patients who found that practising hatha yoga made them feel more relaxed, less stressed out, and less anxious.

Other things that can help you at bad moments

In addition to the above, there are various simple 'self-help' techniques that can help you in moments of great stress or high anxiety. They're pretty commonsense things, but I will briefly list them here. All of these are better than popping tranquillizers:

- Have a nice warm bath; a bath is one of the human race's greatest inventions, and it's first rate for relieving muscular *and* mental stress.
- Have a hot drink; while taking in too much caffeine can make you nervous or 'jumpy', a traditional British 'cuppa' can do wonders in restoring calmness and peace of mind. A *mild* coffee is good too, and so are all those reassuring bedtime drinks that many of us associate with early childhood.
- Have sex; provided that it's safe, uncomplicated sex, carrying no emotional baggage or hang-ups, a gentle spot of sexual activity

– culminating in an orgasm – can be just the thing for making someone feel less stressed and less anxious.

- Have a glass of wine (just one!); although you shouldn't attempt to treat anxiety and stress with large or regular doses of alcohol, nevertheless in moments of difficulty a glass of wine – or some other form of tipple – can be quite therapeutic.
- Talk to a friend or loved one about the problem; when the going gets rough, it's often a great help to 'spill the beans' to someone sympathetic.

Things to avoid

This chapter has been about 'self-help' measures in coping with stress, anxiety or worry.

But there are certain really unwise things that people very often do in an attempt to get relief from their problems. The following will probably make things worse, and are certainly bad for your health:

- drinking alcohol regularly and/or excessively
- smoking
- using 'recreational' drugs
- having promiscuous or dangerous sex – like suddenly deciding to go to bed with your best friend's spouse.

Seeking professional help

So, this chapter has listed all the ways of helping yourself, but there are often times when you need assistance from a health professional in order to defeat stress, worry or anxiety. The various types of professional help are outlined in the next chapter.

10

Professional help and psychological treatments

In the last two chapters we've discussed ways in which you can avoid stress, anxiety and worry, and also ways in which you yourself can re-train your body and mind to cope with these problems.

But what if that isn't enough? What if you need professional help to overcome your difficulties?

Well, it's fortunate that these days there is a lot of such help available. And you shouldn't be at all reluctant about seeking it out, either privately or (where possible) on the NHS.

Traditionally, the British have been very reluctant to ask for psychological assistance. The same is true of certain other nationalities, notably the Irish, the Australians and New Zealanders. In all these countries, people have tended to grow up with the belief that if you have emotional or psychological difficulties, you should just keep quiet about them!

The situation is very different in large parts of the USA, where it has long been socially acceptable to have a therapist to help you deal with the difficulties in your life.

However, the UK's 'stiff upper lip' attitude is slowly changing. In 2010, a survey sponsored by the British Association for Counselling and Psychotherapy (BACP) revealed that:

- Some 94 per cent of people now say that it is 'acceptable' to have counselling or psychotherapy for anxiety and related disorders.
- This figure has shot up since 2004, when it was only 67 per cent.
- Approximately 85 per cent of the public think it's acceptable to have some form of therapy after a divorce or a relationship breakdown.
- Also, 88 per cent of people believe that counselling and psychotherapy should be available on the NHS.
- Over 90 per cent of those surveyed said it is now 'more acceptable to talk [to a professional] about emotional problems than it was in the past'.

All this, says the BACP, 'represents a significant shift in people's attitudes towards therapy – practically a revolution'. The Association thinks that about 250,000 people in the UK are currently having some sort of professional therapy.

So you needn't feel shy about asking for psychological help when you are in trouble with stress, anxiety or worry.

But what *sort* of help ought you to choose? Because so many people know very little about the different types available, I'm going to give a brief outline of them in this chapter. But cognitive behavioural therapy (CBT), which is currently the most widespread and important one, will be explained more fully in Chapter 11.

The main types of help that you can get are as follows:

- counselling
- psychotherapy
- cognitive behavioural therapy (CBT)
- behaviour therapy
- psychodynamic (analytic) therapy
- cognitive analytic therapy
- gestalt therapy
- person-centred therapy
- rational emotive behaviour therapy (REBT)
- coaching (life coaching)
- neuro-linguistic programming (NLP)
- online or computerized psychotherapy
- Improving Access to Psychological Therapy (IAPT) (this is a new NHS scheme – see below).

Let's have a brief look at each of them in turn.

Counselling

Anyone with any sense can see that there are times in life when advice from an experienced person can help you. That's really what counselling is.

Unfortunately, at present there is nothing to prevent anyone describing himself or herself as a 'counsellor'. You yourself could put up a notice in your front garden tomorrow, saying that you are available for 'counselling sessions' – and the law couldn't touch you!

Incidentally, it's a mistake to think that all the people who advertise in *Yellow Pages* and similar directories *must* be well qualified as counsellors. That isn't true at all; the fact is that if they can pay the subscription, they get in the book. Indeed, I've known one or two pretty hopeless characters who somehow got themselves listed in local trade directories under the heading 'Counselling & Advice'.

Also, you'll find that some of those who are listed in these local directories aren't exactly the sort of people who you need to help you with stress, anxiety and worry. In some cases, a careful inspection of their adverts reveals that what they really want to do is to take over your debts! Others rather mysteriously specialize in tarot cards and fortune-telling.

Similarly, if you're looking on the internet for a counsellor, take great care that you pick one who is genuine, and also good at the job. A useful tip is to look for membership of a respected professional organization, such as:

- The British Association for Counselling and Psychotherapy (BACP)
- The British Association for Behavioural and Cognitive Psychotherapies (BABCP)
- The Association for Family Therapy (AFP)
- The UK Council for Psychotherapy (UKCP)
- The College of Sexual and Relationship Therapists (COSRT), formerly The British Association for Sexual and Relationship Therapy (BASRT).

Alternatively, your GP may be able to recommend a sensible local counselling service. A surprisingly small proportion of family doctors actually have a trained counsellor attached to the practice, available to see patients free on the NHS. And the pressure on these helpful people is such that very often they have long waiting lists, and can only take you on for a limited number of sessions.

Amazingly, a few GPs still tell their patients that they 'don't believe in all that counselling stuff'. If you have such a doctor, it might be a good idea to switch to another one.

In general, a good counsellor will do two things:

- Listen to what you say.
- Offer commonsense guidance as to what you should do.

An effective counsellor can certainly be a great help in dealing with stress, anxiety or worry.

Psychotherapy

Psychotherapy is defined in dictionaries as 'the use of psychological methods to treat disorders of the mind'. And that includes stress, anxiety and worry.

Regrettably, at the moment there is a good deal of confusion about precisely what constitutes 'counselling' and what constitutes 'psychotherapy'. A glance at local directories will show you that many practitioners describe themselves as both counsellors *and* psychotherapists. There's certainly quite an overlap, and it's often quite impossible to establish a clear demarcation between psychotherapy and counselling.

One possible point of differentiation is training. Many psychotherapists have taken quite extensive postgraduate instruction. Traditionally, counsellors haven't needed such a long period of training, but some may have undertaken quite a lot anyway.

In the UK, an important factor is that many members of the public would be very reluctant to go and consult a psychotherapist (or indeed *any* professional whose job description began with the prefix 'psych-'). But they'd be quite happy to see someone who is just described as a 'counsellor'!

Unfortunately, there is no *legal* definition of the word 'psychotherapist' at the moment, and in the UK the current situation is that absolutely anyone can call himself or herself a 'psychotherapist'. This will probably change very soon, when appropriate legislation is brought in.

Psychotherapists may specialize in all sorts of areas, notably CBT (see below) and analytic methods. Others may have a particular interest in relationship problems, marriage counselling, sexual dysfunctions, and difficulties with alcohol and other drugs.

You may well have to pay quite lot for psychotherapy: at least £40 an hour, and perhaps three times that in the Harley Street area of London. But fortunately, there is now more (free) psychotherapy treatment available on the NHS than ever before. The reason for this is that during the period 2007 to 2010, the government poured a lot of money into rapidly training some thousands of new therapists, who are supposed to be able to operate simple therapeutic strategies to help patients with anxiety, stress and other disorders.

These developments occurred under a scheme known as Improving Access to Psychological Therapies (IAPT – please see below), and I hope that it won't suffer too much from the cuts that are being implemented from 2010 onwards.

Cognitive behavioural therapy (CBT)

During the first part of the twenty-first century, the type of therapy that has really blossomed in the Western world is cognitive behavioural therapy – or CBT as it is more often called. In the UK, this is partly because of the money that the government has put into it, especially under the IAPT initiative.

Because CBT is now so very important and so very widespread, I'll be devoting the next chapter (Chapter 11) to it. But, in summary, it's a way of teaching people to control their thoughts, so as to improve their mood, and thus help them defeat stresses, anxieties and worries.

Behaviour therapy

Behaviour therapy (sometimes called 'behaviourist therapy') is one of the 'ancestors' or predecessors of CBT.

It's a form of psychotherapy that doesn't dig around in your past or your early childhood, but just attempts to deal with the 'here and now'. The psychotherapist concentrates on helping you to deal with your problems in a practical way. For instance, do you have a frightening phobia about something? Well, the therapist will show you how to overcome your fear and panic through breathing and relaxation exercises.

She may then use 'desensitization' techniques in order to accustom you very gradually to the feared object or situation. Alternatively, with your permission, she might perhaps use 'implosion' to bring you into sudden and complete contact with the frightening thing. The classic example of this is getting a person with arachnophobia to stand in a cage full of spiders – and find out that it's not too bad after all. Not surprisingly, this isn't often done...

Psychodynamic ('analytic') therapy

In the first half of the twentieth century, the treatment of psychological problems was of course very heavily influenced by the work of Freud and his followers. As you probably know, Sigmund Freud (1856–1939) believed that the correct approach to these problems was to analyse (or 'psychoanalyse') the patient.

This was done by putting the person on a couch several times a week, and encouraging him or her to pour out everything that came into his or her mind. There was great emphasis on exploring recollections of early childhood, and particularly memories of traumatic events that might have happened during that period. The basic idea was to explore conflicts that occur in the unconscious mind, and so resolve them.

This technique became known as 'the dynamic (or psychodynamic) method'. It's the kind of therapy that has become embedded in the public consciousness, thanks to all those cartoons of a patient lying on a couch in a New York consulting room, with a bearded man sitting in a chair behind the patient's head, writing everything down in a notebook. Invariably, a diploma hangs on the wall above the couch.

In reality, these days hardly anyone (outside of Manhattan or Beverly Hills) undergoes full-blown psychoanalysis. For a start, it would take up far too much of most people's time – probably two hours, twice or three times a week, for several years. The cost is enormous. And simple calculation shows that the average psychoanalyst would only be able to have about ten patients on his books at any one time. So he'd be fully booked up for years ahead!

However, Freud's ideas, and those of his (temporary) collaborators, Adler and Jung, have influenced an enormous number of health professionals, and a lot of today's psychotherapists are willing to help you with what I would describe as a 'modified' analytic approach.

So, they will try to get to the root of your stresses, anxieties and worries by encouraging you to talk about your feelings, your background and your past. They may possibly ask you to lie on a couch, or maybe just sit in a comfortable chair. And they will probably say very little during your sessions, simply letting you do the talking – and seeing what emerges.

Not altogether surprisingly, this type of psychotherapy is now fairly rare in the NHS, but it's sometimes possible to obtain it on a short-term basis – maybe for six or twelve sessions.

Cognitive analytic therapy

Cognitive analytic therapy (CAT) is essentially a fairly short-duration treatment that combines the ideas of CBT with those of analysis. It was developed in the UK during the latter part of the twentieth century by Dr Anthony Ryle.

Therapists start by trying to find out why a person's stresses and anxieties have occurred, going back to childhood if necessary, in a rather analytic way (see above). Then they attempt to help the person to apply the methods of CBT to solving the problems.

CAT is not all that widely available in the UK, but there is now a professional association of therapists who carry it out. You'll find it at: <www.acat.me.uk>.

Gestalt therapy

Gestalt therapy tends to be mentioned a lot in erudite novels, and in Sunday newspaper supplements, but in fact it's now quite uncommon in the UK. The German word *Gestalt* means 'shape', 'form', 'figure' or 'stature'. But in psychological usage in the UK and the USA it is employed to mean 'as a whole' or 'holistic'.

So gestalt therapy, which is alleged to trace some of its origins to the works of Goethe and Kant, tries to help you by concentrating on the whole of your present experience, as well as yourself, and the environment you live in, plus your relationship with your therapist.

One intriguing aspect of gestalt is its use of the 'open chair' technique, in which the psychotherapist encourages you to imagine that someone (say, your father or mother) is sitting in the chair in front of you. You can then tell that person what you really think of him or her, and voice thoughts that you were unable to express in the past. This can be a pretty emotional business, but it may help get rid of stresses and anxieties.

Person-centred therapy

This therapy (which is also known as 'Rogerian therapy', after Carl Rogers, who invented it in the mid-twentieth century) is particularly good for those whose stresses, worries and anxieties are linked to poor self-esteem.

The general idea is that the therapist does her best to demonstrate genuine interest, empathy and unconditional encouragement towards the client. At the centre of the treatment is the notion that if a person is cared for and respected – even if only by his therapist – then that person begins to feel improved self-esteem. He should therefore have less need to feel stressed and anxious.

One obvious drawback of this major school of psychotherapy is the fact that a therapist might find that she simply cannot stand her client! However, there is a lot more to Rogerian therapy than I've been able to set out in this brief summary, and if you think it could be for you, then please check out the website of the British Association for the Person-Centred Approach at: <www.bapca.org.uk>.

Rational emotive behaviour therapy (REBT)

It would be fair to describe REBT as a close relative of CBT. It was developed by psychoanalyst Albert Ellis in the mid-twentieth century. It focuses on the fact that all human beings have some rigid and dogmatic beliefs that cause anxiety and stress. These notions are generally caused by irrational thinking.

For instance, absolutist beliefs are sometimes concerned with how well we 'must' do in life. They make the person feel that unless she is absolutely the best at everything, then she has failed badly. Obviously, this can cause enormous stress.

Similarly, a man may seem to be ignored by his boss when they pass in the street. As a result, he could become irrationally convinced that this means that he is a contemptible person, and may soon be fired! He doesn't think of other explanations, such as the possibility that his boss (1) was thinking of something else, or (2) was ill, or (3) was under the influence of alcohol, or (4) was walking along with someone other than his wife.

REBT aims to help clients by challenging them to replace illogical and inflexible beliefs with more sensible ones.

Want to learn more? Then please check out the website of the Association for Rational Emotive Behaviour Therapy (AREBT), at: <http://rebt.bizland.com>.

Coaching (life coaching)

A surprising new development of the first ten years of the twenty-first century was the emergence of the popular coaching (or 'life coaching') movement, as a way of helping people manage their lives. However, I must stress that coaching is not specifically intended to deal with anxiety and worry – though it may well help to reduce stresses, particularly in the field of business.

Indeed, business and commerce have largely 'fuelled' the coaching movement, especially as many companies are willing to pay large sums for their employees to be coached – even in times of recession.

One reason for the movement's current popularity is that fact that its name doesn't *sound* like anything psychological! People who wouldn't want to consult anyone whose job title starts with 'psych-' are very happy to say: 'Oh, I'm just having a couple of hours coaching tonight'.

Life coaches are trained to offer you practical strategies and solutions for reorganizing and improving your life – and particularly the business side of it. Many of them describe themselves as 'corporate' or 'executive' coaches. Others deal specifically with stress management.

Some actually operate by phone or email, which of course should help to keep costs down.

You may find it useful to look at the website of the Association for Coaching, at: <www.associationforcoaching.com>.

Neuro-linguistic programming (NLP)

NLP is a form of psychotherapy which, back in the 1980s and 1990s, became very popular in the Western world. Since then, its star seems to have waned a bit, partly because it has provoked a lot of opposition among more orthodox schools of therapy, and also because it has been involved in a great deal of litigation.

Nowadays, there are many different therapists practising varying kinds of NLP. They generally believe that there is a relationship between a person's neurological processes, his spoken language, and his behaviour.

NLP is defined by various practitioners in different ways, but essentially it is a school of interpersonal communication that is concerned with the link between patterns of thought and successful patterns of behaviour. In the early days, its supporters maintained that it was an effective form of psychological therapy, able to address many common problems, such as phobias and psychosomatic illnesses. But in recent years, practitioners of other disciplines have suggested that its claims are not borne out by scientific results.

Online or computerized psychotherapy

In this computer age, it was inevitable that some therapists would attempt to treat clients by email. This can be done, and it's certainly less costly than traditional therapy is.

However, 'electronic consultations' do have the major drawback that it is difficult for the psychotherapist to pick up the hints and clues that people normally give out when they are talking to someone in a consulting room.

A further recent development has been the introduction of therapy by computer program. That may sound a little odd, but in fact it is possible for a person who has anxieties and stresses to 'talk' to a cleverly designed program that elicits answers and then gives advice. Quite a lot of men and women actually enjoy this sort of 'computer consultation'.

So far, most of the work on this technology has been based on the principles of CBT (see the next chapter). Currently, there are two major programs available free on the NHS in England and Wales. One of them ('Beating the Blues') is really intended for people with depression, but the other, which is called 'FearFighter', is intended for those who have phobias or other anxieties, or post-traumatic stress.

Please note two things:

- The 'FearFighter' program has to be *prescribed* by a doctor who is authorized to do so; you can't just go into it off your own bat. More details at <www.fearfighter.com>.
- It's important not to confuse 'FearFighter' with an American device of the same name, which is alleged to reduce anxiety and stress by passing small electric currents into your head; I do not recommend that you purchase one of these devices.

In addition, in Scotland there is a free CBT-style course, designed by a professor of psychiatry (Chris Williams), and open, without charge, to anyone anywhere who wants to try it. You'll find it at: <www.livinglife-tothefull.com>.

Much of the work on providing 'e-therapy' has been produced under the UK government's Improving Access to Psychological Therapy scheme (see below).

Improving Access to Psychological Therapy (IAPT)

In 2006–7, the British government came up with a plan called 'Improving Access to Psychological Therapy', in order to try to help many more of the large number of people who suffer from anxiety, stress and other psychological disorders.

The government promised to invest a great deal of money in it, and the general idea was that as cognitive behavioural therapy (CBT) seemed to be so cost-effective, it should be the basis of the new plan.

To be frank, very little happened for a couple of years, but by 2010 the scheme was really beginning to 'come on stream'. So effective has it been that in some areas of the UK, NHS waiting lists for 'talking therapy' have become very short. Indeed, a couple of *private* psycho-therapists in London's Harley Street area have said to me recently that they are no longer seeing as many clients, because 'the NHS is doing a much better job than it used to'.

The essentials of the IAPT scheme are as follows:

- The NHS is training a huge number of new-style CBT therapists – probably 10,000 eventually.
- Some of these are people who already have a background in psychology, counselling, nursing or mental health, and it was announced in August 2010 that they will take on quite complex treatments, and now be called 'High Intensity Therapy Workers'.
- Bright and empathetic people from a range of backgrounds are also

being given short-course CBT training to become 'Psychological Wellbeing Practitioners'.

- As they qualify in simple psychotherapy, all these people are starting to see patients in one-to-one situations, and also in workshops and as part of group therapy.
- Some of them are going to be involved in helping patients via computerized CBT therapy.
- A number of patients may access the new service themselves, but most will be referred to it by GPs or their staff.

It looks as though this new CBT scheme will help a lot of people in England and Wales who have problems with stress, anxiety and worry. But naturally, much depends on how the economic situation progresses – and whether the funding is continued.

North of the border, NHS Education Scotland is bringing forward a scheme called 'Increasing the Availability of Evidence-Based Psychological Therapies', which should make CBT and other 'talking' treatments much more widely used. The Scottish government plans to have this scheme well under way by April 2011.

And in Northern Ireland, the Health Minister announced in June 2010 that a new Psychological Services strategy, including CBT, as well as behavioural treatment, counselling, family support and psychoanalytic therapy, would soon benefit 'hundreds of people'.

If you'd like to know more about cognitive behavioural therapy (CBT), then please read the next chapter.

11

Cognitive Behavioural Therapy (CBT)

As we saw in the last chapter, in the early part of the twenty-first century, cognitive behavioural therapy (CBT) became the dominating force in the treatment of stress, anxiety and worry. This has happened in the UK, Ireland, the USA, Australia, New Zealand, Canada, and indeed France (where it's known as 'TCC', short for *Thérapie Comportementale et Cognitive*).

There are two main reasons why CBT has become so popular:

- You can have it as a short course, so it doesn't 'drag on' for years.
- It works.

Admittedly, it may *not* work for absolutely everybody, but very large numbers of people have found that after a course of, say, six or twelve CBT sessions, their anxieties and stresses have become much more manageable.

So what exactly is it?

It's a system in which the therapist teaches you that, to a very large extent, your thoughts control your moods. And so, if you can alter your way of thinking, your mood will improve, your anxiety, worry and stress will recede, and your life will probably become substantially happier.

Epictetus

Now the idea that your thoughts control how you feel is a brilliantly simple one. The first person who came up with this notion was a Greek slave called Epictetus (AD 55 to about AD 135), who was working in Rome when he somehow managed to establish his own branch of philosophy. Among his main teachings were the following:

- Some things in life are simply not under our control.
- The most important thing in life is self-knowledge.
- We are responsible for our own actions and thoughts.
- We can control our thoughts by self-discipline.

- Suffering arises from trying to control what is uncontrollable, or neglecting what is within our power.
- It's not life's events that upset us – it's our *view* of them.

The idea that humans can alter their perception of life by simply controlling their own thoughts turns up throughout the centuries in the writings of many others, notably Shakespeare, who says in *Hamlet*: 'There is nothing either good or bad, but thinking makes it so.' This idea appears repeatedly in his plays.

And in the middle of the twentieth century, the same belief led to the development of CBT in the USA, mainly by Dr Aaron Beck. He was a psychoanalyst who realized that quite often analysis alone was not working, because 'negative thoughts' were holding his patients back.

Negative thoughts

What sort of negative thoughts? Well, Beck spotted that a lot of people's minds were clogged up with unhelpful ideas. These can be things like:

- 'I'd be no good at that'.
- 'People dislike me'.
- 'I'm hopeless at maths/English/conversation/sex/getting on with people/whatever'.
- 'I'm unlovable'.
- 'My bottom always looks fat, and always will'.
- 'I'm just not good enough'.

He decided that when men and women dwell on these pointless and disabling ideas, their mood plummets. And they're liable to become anxious, phobic, panicky or stressed. Therefore, he developed a system of treatment in which people are encouraged to:

- think more logically about themselves;
- think more rationally about the world.

So the idea is that the therapist can help you change the way you *think* (that's how the word 'cognitive' comes into it), and how you subsequently *behave* (that's the 'behavioural' bit).

You may feel a bit cynical, and say: 'Oh, that could never work for *me*'. But please read on, because I assure you that CBT does seem to help most people.

Let's have a look at one man's story:

Tom

Tom was a manager, working for a firm that had recently been taken over, and his life was now full of stress and worry. He was troubled by several quite disabling anxiety symptoms, like trembling, tummy-rumbling, and sudden breathlessness when he got up to speak at meetings.

After trying various tranquillizers without success, he eventually found his way to a CBT therapist. She listened sympathetically to his account of his problems, which had clearly started when his company was taken over.

She got him to relax and discuss his feelings. Before long, she was able to identify the stressful thoughts that were going round and round in his brain. She also picked up on several quite irrational statements that he made to her – things like: 'If I don't do well in this job, I'll be a failure', and 'I really *have to* stay in this post, at all costs', and 'If I lose this job, my family will starve'.

Towards the end of their first session together, she got him to look at the sheer *lack of evidence* for some of his negative thoughts. And she was able to show him that these illogical thoughts were making him unhappy.

At the end of the hour, she sent him off with some 'homework' to do (see below). And over the next few weeks, she guided him into thinking much more positively. In fact, he became so positive that he resigned from the job, and got a better one.

At the end of six sessions of CBT, he was a very much happier and more relaxed man. Even more importantly, he'd learned ways of challenging irrational thinking – ways that he'd be able to use again and again in different situations for the rest of his life.

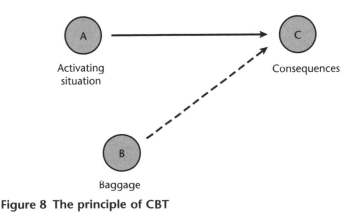

Figure 8 The principle of CBT

This story illustrates the basic principles of CBT. If you can manage to alter the way in which you think about things, then your stresses, anxieties and worries will recede – and a trained therapist can help you do this.

Look at Figure 8, and you'll see more precisely what I mean:

A represents the 'Activating Situation' which seems to cause the person's problems (like his firm going bust, or his spouse leaving him).
B represents the 'Baggage' that we all carry in our minds (that is, the irrational beliefs that we have inside ourselves).
C represents the 'Consequences' caused by the interaction of A and B (for example, stress, anxiety and worry).

In general, people assume that A is the cause of C. In other words, they believe that external events lead to such consequences as stress-related illnesses or anxiety states or endless worrying. But in reality a good deal of the problem is a result of the fact that B (the emotional baggage and irrational thoughts in our minds) is creating the trouble at point C. And if the therapist can help people get rid of all that illogical baggage, then life will be a great deal better.

What to expect from a session of CBT

What will happen if you opt for CBT? Well, it won't be anything like the 'psychological' set-up that you've probably seen in a hundred films and cartoons, and that we mentioned earlier in the book, where the patient lies back on a couch and talks about his early childhood, and how his mother deprived him of his favourite dummy.

Instead, the therapist will invite you to sit on a comfortable chair, and will then ask you to talk about your problems. She'll probably sit in a casual chair herself; very few CBT therapists position themselves behind the 'barrier' of a desk.

She will listen carefully to what you say, and take notes. She's unlikely to ask you questions about your infancy or childhood. What she's primarily interested in is what's going on *now*. In particular, she will want to know how you *feel* about things.

Most sessions last for an hour, so you have plenty of time to talk. By the end of the first appointment, your therapist will probably have started to show you how to think along more rational, useful and positive lines than you've been doing up till now. (Though, curiously enough, CBT therapists don't usually use the word 'positive'.)

At the end of the session, she may well give you some 'homework' – in the shape of a questionnaire, or perhaps a chart on which she wants you to record all your negative and harmful thoughts during the next week. Not everybody manages to complete this task. They sometimes say that they're 'too busy' or 'too stressed'!

But whether you've done the homework or not, go back next time. CBT therapists usually see people about once a week. And, generally speaking, by the end of six weeks or so, you should be feeling quite a bit better.

How do you find yourself a CBT therapist?

Until recently, I'd have said that it would be very difficult to find yourself a CBT therapist free on the NHS, and that if you *did* find one, you'd have to wait a long time for an appointment.

But things are looking a lot better at the time of writing, because of the new 'Improved Access to Psychological Therapies' schemes that I mentioned in the previous chapter.

So, at the moment, it's well worth asking your GP to refer you to your local psychological services. Provided that NHS funding doesn't dry up too much, they should be able to arrange for you to consult a CBT therapist fairly near you. You'll probably be seen on a 'one-to-one' basis, but in some areas of the UK there is a tendency for the therapist to get people together in small groups or workshops.

You might perhaps feel unhappy about discussing your stresses and anxieties with other people. If so, say so. But recently I've been surprised to find that quite a few men and women actually *like* talking things over with others, and comparing their reactions to various causes of stress. In fact, after the end of one course, the group actually met up later for a reunion in a pub.

Private CBT therapy

Despite the improved facilities offered by the NHS, many people prefer to see a psychotherapist privately.

There are various reasons for this. Notably, some people feel that consulting a private therapist is their own 'secret'. It doesn't involve their GP or anybody else. Indeed, it's most unlikely that the CBT therapist will even write to your doctor, unless you specifically ask her to. And not a word of what you tell her will ever appear on your NHS notes, or on any government-run computer.

So how do you find a private therapist? You can search on the internet, or in local trade directories, looking out for psychotherapists who state that they are members of the British Association for Behavioural and Cognitive Therapies (BABCP). Or you can simply check out the website of the BABCP at: <www.babcp.org.uk> and then click on 'Find a Therapist'.

What about costs? These vary a great deal, depending on what part of the UK you live in. That may seem surprising, but when you think about it (a very cognitive thing to do!), fees are likely to depend on the rents and rates that the therapist has to pay.

So if you pick a therapist who is practising from her own front room in the suburbs of a small town, you might find she charges about £40 a session. But if you choose someone who works in London's Harley Street or Wimpole Street, you may well be looking at over £100 per hour.

Regrettably, health insurance companies don't often pay out for 'psychotherapy' fees, but it may be worth checking your policy, just in case. Finally, a very few enlightened employers will obligingly pay for valued employees to see a CBT therapist. This mainly occurs in the public sector.

Other ways of using CBT

Most cognitive behavioural therapy happens face-to-face in a quiet consulting room, but it is also possible to get help in other ways.

For instance, CBT does lend itself reasonably well to 'online' therapy. There's more information about that – including the names of a couple of websites that you can try out – in Chapter 10.

Also, some CBT experts say that it is possible to help yourself through books and CD-ROMs, and that may well be true. However, I feel that if you are in a lot of distress it's very helpful and comforting to have your own therapist with whom you can talk things through.

Mindfulness

Finally, let me tell you a little about 'mindfulness'. You'll probably hear this word quite a bit in the future, because the idea of 'mindfulness' has suddenly become fashionable. Many therapists, and particularly CBT ones, state that they use mindfulness in treating clients. There's now actually a branch of cognitive therapy called 'MBCT' – which stands for 'Mindfulness-Based Cognitive Therapy'.

Research published during the period 2000–10 has strongly suggested that it helps in reducing stress and anxiety. But what on earth is it? Well, it's a notion that has gradually developed from Buddhism. CBT experts and others employ it as a technique in which they help their clients to get into a state of mind in which they live and focus 'in the moment' – to the exclusion of everything else.

Personally, I would describe it as a form of brief meditation, in which you spend a few minutes in thinking about one particular thing, focusing all your awareness on it. Instead of dwelling on your problems, you devote your mind solely to this one object.

CBT therapists are particularly likely to use mindfulness in the form of what's called 'the raisin technique'. It was developed by Toronto psychotherapist Professor Zindel Segal and his colleagues. Maybe to start with it will strike you as quite crazy, but a lot of over-stressed and anxious people say that it helps them. What happens is this:

- The therapist gets out a packet of raisins, and selects one.
- She asks you to hold it in your hand, and to look at it as if you've never seen one before.
- She gets you to look at it searchingly, noticing how many grooves it has, and which way they run. She also asks you to note the colour of it, and whether the shade varies in different places.
- Then she asks you to *feel* it, probably with your eyes closed. Is it smooth or rough or sticky? What sensations do you get when you roll it between finger and thumb?
- Next, she may get you to lift it to your nose, and inhale. What do you notice about its scent?
- Then, she'll probably ask you to put the raisin in your mouth, beginning by placing it on your tongue. How does it feel? What sensations do you experience as you roll it around?
- After that, she may get you to bite into it slowly. How does it taste? You focus on the experience of its flavour, as the juices gradually reach your taste buds.
- Finally, you swallow the raisin, noting the pleasant feeling as it leaves your mouth and heads down towards your stomach.
- Afterwards, you breathe in and out deeply, while you think about the sight, feel, smell and taste of the little raisin.

It's easy to think that the raisin technique is like something out of 'Pseuds' Corner' in the magazine *Private Eye*. It's certainly not a technique that all of us would be eager to try. But, for many people, it's a peaceful, relaxing exercise that soothes the troubled brain, and as part of CBT therapy, it can work very well.

Summing up

Cognitive behavioural therapy is definitely 'flavour of the month' at present, especially because of all the money that the UK government has poured into it.

There are experts who are opposed to it, saying that it has claimed more than it can deliver. One consultant psychiatrist has stated publicly that CBT has 'hoodwinked' the government, and that the authorities have been 'seduced by its apparent cheapness'.

Time will tell whether the current massive investment in CBT will pay off. But for *you*, as a person who is presumably distressed by anxiety, worry or stress, I would say that it is well worth trying. Good luck.

Index